RVing

Less Hassle—More Joy

Secrets to Having More Fun with

Your RV—Even on a Limited Budget

Jerry Minchey

www.LifeRV.com

Stony River Media

Minchey, Jerry. RVing Less Hassle—More Joy: Secrets to Having More Fun with Your RV—Even on a Limited Budget / Jerry Minchey 2017 v.1

Published by Stony River Media

Knoxville, TN

StonyRiverMedia.com

ISBN: 978-0-9844968-9-1

Dedicated to my parents, Charles and Helen Minchey.

I am indebted to Anna Edgren, Jill Goldman, Jim Fitzpatrick, Cinnamon Sky, and Ken Darrow, M.A. (Fiverr.com/MrProofreader). Without their editing and proofing this book would not exist—at least not in a format you would want to read.

Contents

Introduction

"You can't buy happiness... but you can buy an RV, and that's pretty close."

~ Anonymous

In 1859, when Charles Dickens wrote, *"It was the best of times, it was the worst of times. . ."* in his classic book *A Tale of Two Cities,* was he talking about living in an RV?

That phrase can pretty well describe spending time in an RV. You can have some wonderful times and some terrible times.

The opening sentence of the book goes on to say, *"It was the age of wisdom, it was the age of foolishness. . ."*

When you're RVing, you can sometimes think buying an RV was a wise decision and sometimes think it was a foolish decision.

So, yes, I think Charles Dickens did a great job of describing the experiences of spending time in an RV. Maybe he didn't intend to, but he sure described the experiences I've had in mine.

How Would You Describe Your RVing Experience?

Are you spending time in your RV (full-time, part-time, or just sometime) and finding that it's more expensive and not as much fun as you expected it to be?

Maybe you're finding there's more hassle than you expected. Something is always breaking, leaking, malfunctioning, or just plain causing you a pain in the butt.

It would be nice if there were a few hacks, techniques, or gadgets that you could find that would make all of the frustrating things go away, so you could enjoy RVing the way it seems like everyone else is doing.

There are plenty of seemingly happy, carefree RVers traveling around the country, writing blogs and not having any of the hassles, stress, and frustrations (and expenses) that you're having to deal with.

Most of the RVing blogs make it out to be a utopia. What do they know that you don't know—or are they just faking it?

In other words, in the real world you're finding that RVing is not as much fun, not as inexpensive, and not the stress-free adventure you were expecting.

All Is Not Lost

If this describes your RVing experiences, all is not lost. There's a way that you can enjoy RVing with less hassle, and more joy, just as the title of this book promises.

The purpose of this book is to reveal the secrets to having more fun with your RV and doing it on a limited budget.

There are 8.9 million RVs in the United States. Some people live full time in their RVs, some live full time part of the time (for example, winters in Florida or Arizona) and, of course, many people use their RVs for vacation and for weekend getaways.

In other words. . .

There Is No One Right Way to RV

RVs range in size from tiny pop-ups to the mega 45-foot, Class A rigs. They each serve a different market and a different purpose.

We all start out as RV newbies. We learn from each other, and we learn a lot the hard way.

If you spend enough time driving a motorhome or dragging a fifth wheel or travel trailer across the country, you'll sooner or later learn a lot about how to enjoy RVing.

In this book I want to help you speed up that learning process.

You Don't Have to Learn Everything the Hard Way

I have been living full time in my motorhome for four years. I've learned a lot (some things I learned the hard way) and I continue to learn new hacks and techniques all the time. You can never learn them all.

There are several books out there for newbies that explain the pros and cons of living the RV lifestyle and guide RV wannabes who are considering embarking on the RV lifestyle.

In fact, I have written five of those books. You can see them listed at the end of this book. If you're already into RVing, you may have read some of my books. If you have, I thank you.

This is not another RVing book for newbies or for RVing wannabees. This book is for the 8.9 million people who are already living the RVing adventure—either full time, part time, or sometime. If that describes you . . .

Let's Get Started

Experiencing the ultimate RVing adventures is not just a matter of learning a lot of hacks and techniques. Learning some of these things will add to your joy, but that's not the ultimate answer.

The Most Important Thing When It Comes to Experiencing the Ultimate Joy of RVing is Attitude.

Not everything is going to go right. You have to learn to expect and accept things going wrong.

And by the way, some of the things that go wrong will be expensive. That's why you need an emergency fund. We'll talk more about that later.

When people think about taking a trip in their RV, one of the things they think about is getting away from it all and living a stress-free life.

You Can't Have the Ultimate RVing Experience If You're Feeling Constant Stress

I have a whole chapter about how to eliminate most stress and how to deal with the stress that you can't eliminate. We'll get to that later.

Things are always going wrong when you live in an RV, and that's true whether you're in your RV for one week or full time. There's always something to deal with. It's part of the journey.

I had my annual physical this past week. When the doctor looked at my blood work and saw that my numbers were all well within the good range and saw that my cholesterol was 125 (below 200 is ideal) and my LDL cholesterol (the bad or lethal cholesterol) was at 56 (anything below 100 is considered good), he said, "I don't think I've ever seen LDL cholesterol that low. You must be living a very low-stress lifestyle."

I explained that I was living full time in my motorhome, and for the last month I had been camping next to a river in the mountains, and there was no one parked nearby. He said, "That explains it."

A friend of mine asked, "Did you also tell him that you weren't married?"

The title of the ever-popular book (published more than 20 years ago and still selling well), *Don't Sweat the Small Stuff, and It's All Small Stuff* pretty well describes the attitude you need in order to enjoy your RV. Maybe the author, Richard Carlson, had RVing in mind when he wrote that book.

Sometimes Trouble Can Be Fun

I was talking with one of my many cousins the other day. Back when he was about 10 years old, two of his uncles had old flatbed trucks and from time to time they would haul watermelons or tobacco (or whatever they could get a job hauling).

There were not many regulations back then like there are now. My cousin said that sometimes he would get to ride along on some of their shorter one-day trips.

He confessed to me that he always hoped something would go wrong (and usually it did). They would have a flat or a fan belt would break or a radiator hose would spring a leak. It was a lot more fun and exciting if they had some kind of trouble.

I can see how "trouble" would be exciting for a young boy, and how it would add more adventure to the trip, but as RVers, we don't wish for trouble to happen. Maybe if we did, we would be expecting it and things breaking wouldn't stress us out so much.

So, yes, sometimes trouble can be fun—at least for a young boy, but not for us RVers.

Happiness Is a Matter of Attitude

A lot of people like their big RV, and in the winter they like to camp where it's warm, but for Kim Huber Buzan, her favorite way to camp is in the snow in her tiny Airstream.

The picture below of her cozy RV almost makes me want to camp in the snow. Notice that I said, "almost." I like Florida in the winter months. I don't like snow.

For some people this is the perfect way to camp

Yes, happiness is a matter of attitude. And if you think about it, you have complete control over your attitude (or at least you should have).

Many people love small RVs. I know a lot more people who have sold their big RV and bought a smaller one than I know who have sold their small RV and gone with a larger one.

Keeping up with the Joneses is basically non-existent in the RV world. More than likely most of your life you were always wanting a bigger house, a nicer car, and more of the latest "stuff."

The advertising media have done a good job of making us unhappy with what we have, and of convincing us to always want more.

Most RVers (at least the ones who are the happiest) have learned that in many cases having less makes them happier than having more.

The information in this book comes from my own experiences and from many hours of sitting around campfires talking to other RVers. I hope you find the information helpful.

Bottom line: To sum it up, in order to have less stress when you're RVing, you'll need a few gadgets, a few apps, you'll need to learn a few hacks, change a few routines, and implement a few new techniques (and I'll show you how to do all of that in this book).

But the most important thing is that you will need to change your attitude about a few things—not many, just a few.

All of this can be done easily and quickly. This book will explain how to make it happen.

Chapter 1:

Stress and Joy Can't Coexist

"If you ask what is the single most important key to longevity, I would have to say it is avoiding worry, stress and tension. And if you didn't ask me, I'd still have to say it."

~ George Burns

Whether you're heading off on a weekend adventure, a family vacation, a winter in Arizona or Florida, or maybe even hitting the road to try full-time RVing, it's easy to get stressed out with all of the hassles that seem to always go along with RVing.

11

After all, there is a lot to worry about and there are many things that could (and probably will) go wrong.

On top of worrying about the things that might happen, and thinking about the things you forgot to bring, there could always be squeaks and rattles getting on your nerves, and there may be kids who are energetic and full of excitement, and pets that won't settle down. It's easy to ask, "How can I relax?"

It's hard to find joy when you're dealing with hassle and stress. In fact, I would say that it's impossible to fully find joy if you can't relax.

Let's start at the beginning and take one thing at a time. Problems (or potential problems) can generally be divided into one of two groups—things that can be solved by money and things that can't be solved by money.

If money will solve the problem, you don't have a problem—except working out how you get the money. And here's how to get the money.

Living Below Your Means Can Give You More Money and More Joy

Living below your means is one of the best ways to reduce the stress in your life because when you live below your means, you will have money for the unexpected things that are sure to happen.

That's why you start out RVing with an emergency fund. Then, when something breaks, there's no stress. You have the money; you get it fixed and you go on.

"The secret of happiness, you see, is not found in seeking more, but in developing the capacity to enjoy less."

~ Socrates

Socrates died in 399 BC. I don't know if the concept of stress even existed back then, but he sure nailed it in describing how to be happy. I think his comment would apply equally well to reducing (or even eliminating) stress.

All of this sounds great, but to make it really work, you have to start by owning an RV you can afford. That's easier to do than you might think.

But since you're reading this book, you probably already own an RV. Hopefully, you didn't spend more than you can afford (or have payments that don't leave you much money for traveling), but what is done is done, so let's go on.

Other Ways to Eliminate Stress

One of the best ways to eliminate a lot of stress is to follow the advice in this Polish proverb:

Every time you feel yourself being pulled into other people's nonsense, repeat these words, "Not my circus, not my monkeys."

Another thing that causes stress is having too much to do and always being behind. We all tend to take on too much.

I like Warren Buffet's technique of saying "No" to almost everything. He said. . .

"If it's not a Hell Yes, it's a NO."

Adopt this attitude and you will free up a lot of time, and you won't be stressed out because you have agreed to do too many things.

Bottom line: You have to find ways to eliminate stress before you can truly experience the joy of spending time in your RV. The more stress you can eliminate, the more joy you will experience.

Now that you know the problem, in the rest of this book I'm going to show you ways to make this happen.

Chapter 2:

Attitude Is the Key to Enjoying the RVing Adventure

"The greatest discovery of my generation is that a human being can alter his life by altering his attitude."

~ William James

When I think about attitude, I think about the story of Tom Sawyer whitewashing the fence.

Whether it's a dreaded chore or a fun thing to do all depends on the attitude of the person doing it.

To help you maintain the right attitude, keep the following quote in mind:

"Life is 10% what happens to you and 90% how you react to it."

~ Charles R. Swindoll

We don't have a lot of control over what happens in life (some, of course, but not much). We do have a lot of control over how we react to what happens to us. With practice, maybe we can have even more control over how we react.

Your Attitude Toward Maintenance Is an Example of This Concept

With most insurance policies you can either pay your insurance all in one annual payment or you can pay monthly.

That's the way to look at RV maintenance expenses. Things may go bad a little bit at a time, but you usually don't know it until all of a sudden when something totally fails.

In other words, most maintenance problems hit you all at once, but put some money in your maintenance account each month, and when something expensive happens, you've already paid for it.

Of course, this money is in addition to your emergency fund, which should be for a true emergency and not just for predictable expenses.

Every mile you drive you're using up your gasoline (or diesel fuel). You're also using up your tires, but you pay for tires every few years not a little for every trip.

Even if you took a 500-mile trip and didn't have to spend anything on maintenance, that doesn't mean you didn't get that much closer to having to spend some money on repairs.

One RVer told me that every time he puts $100 worth of gas in his rig he also puts $100 in an envelope that he keeps for maintenance expenses. My maintenance doesn't run to nearly that much, but his technique may not be a bad idea.

That way it's not a stressful situation when something breaks and you have to spend money all of a sudden on repairs.

It's not like you had bad luck on this trip or this month. That would be like saying that you had bad luck when the gas gauge got down close to empty and you had to spend $100 on gas.

You've been using up those tires and your refrigerator all along, it's just that all of a sudden it's time to pay for what you've been using.

This is just one of the ways to keep RVing from being stressful.

Stress Is Not Caused by What Happens, But by How You Deal With What Happens

When you have an unexpected problem, if you have an emergency fund there's no problem—and no stress.

You just take money from your emergency fund to pay for the repairs and on you go.

Of course, if you have an emergency and spend some of the money in your emergency fund, you need to immediately start making arrangements to put money back into your emergency fund to replenish what you took out.

Random Events Are Random—Period

I've seen intelligent people say that, since it's been a long time since they've rolled a 7, they're due to roll a 7. Duh?

Yesterday I was talking to a guy who was cleaning up after a flood. He said that this was a 100-year flood, so he shouldn't see another flood like this during the rest of his lifetime.

Don't get caught looking at situations this way.

Don't think that, since you've already spent money this month repairing your air conditioner, you're less likely to have a tire go bad.

If you find yourself thinking like this, spend some of your maintenance money and go buy a rabbit's foot.

By the way, I'll go into more details about maintenance in Chapter 9. Maintenance is an important subject and a big cause of stress. It needs its own chapter.

Bottom line: The right attitude is important to fully enjoying your RVing adventure. Don't let random events change your attitude. Remember that random events are random—period.

Chapter 3

Your RV Is One of the Family—It Needs a Name

"We are all here on earth to help others; what on earth the others are here for I don't know."

~ W. H. Auden

Your RV should be like your dog—something you love dearly and would never think of getting rid of.

Well, not exactly. It's OK to sell your RV and get a different one that you like better.

You probably wouldn't want to sell your Doberman just because you found a poodle that you like better. But it's OK to sell your Class C RV if you decide you like an Airstream better.

Other than the fact that it's fine to get rid of your RV and get a different kind, think of your RV the same way you would your dog.

One of the best ways to make your RV one of the family is to name it. You wouldn't think of getting a dog and then not giving it a name.

RVers are not as hung up on naming their rig as boat owners are about naming their boats. Boat owners have to have a ceremony to change the name of their boat. And they usually destroy a perfectly good bottle of champagne in the process. We RVers are not so foolish.

When RVers buy a used RV, they don't even know what the previous owner had named the rig, unless of course, it is painted on the RV. And yes, some people do paint the name of their RV on the front or back of their rig.

Pictures of Some RVs that Have a Name

The first one is Brittany and Eric's Class A motorhome that they named *Wanderlust.*

Wanderlust

Next is Chris and Cherie's beautifully converted bus, *Zephyr*. (Look for the name just above the windshield.)

Zephyr

Becky at www.InterstellerOrchard.com didn't paint the name on her rig, but she named her little Casita camper *Cas*. Why not?

Cas

Anna Edgren named her Pace Arrow *"The RV"* since it's the only one in the world—at least, as far as she is concerned it is.

The RV

Names of Other RVs

While reading posts on Facebook and seeing hundreds of RVs in campgrounds, I've compiled a list of RV names I like. Many RV names have stories to go with them. I've added stories below for a few of these names.

Since there are 8.9 million RVs in the US and there are not 8.9 million unique names for RVs, a lot of RVs have the same name. And a lot of RVs don't have names.

If you need help coming up with a name for your RV, maybe this list will help you:

- Tag-along (for a camper)

- The Castle

- Cram-A-Lot Inn

- Wheel-Estate

- Hi-Ho Silver

- Dolly (It's a Newmar Kountry Star model)

- Willie (On the road again)

- Gypsy

- The Beast

- The Fort (Because we all built forts to play in as kids—now we're still playing in a fort.)

- Leap-of-Faith (or just Faith for short)

- Iron Teepee

- Mobile Mansion

- RVie

- Bobby McGee

Naming your RV and making it part of the family will change your attitude towards your rig.

That's important because your RV will be part of your life. It will take care of you and you will have to take care of it. Just like your dog, your RV will need annual checkups, an occasional bath, a lot of feeding (gas), and from time to time there will be trips to the vet (I mean the RV shop).

Don't think of your RV as the enemy or the cause of all of your troubles. (Yes, it will break down or need maintenance at the most inconvenient times. And it will need expensive work done sometimes when it doesn't fit your budget or your schedule. Your kids probably needed braces at a time when it didn't fit into your budget too).

My brother's dog recently had to have surgery for a blocked bladder that cost $1,800 (plus a lot of follow-up visits). Just like your RV, she was one of the family and no one complained about the expense.

Seriously, name your RV, think of it as one of the family, take care of it, and you will both have a wonderful time together.

After You Name Your RV You'll Take Better Care of It

After all, it's one of the family now. Taking care of it will come natural after you name your RV.

As a follow-up note, a lot of RVers (me included) spend many hours doing preventive maintenance themselves. Do a lot of little things every month and then once a year do (or have an RV shop do) at least one major job—like overhauling the brakes, changing the transmission fluid, etc.

Don't wait for things to fail (and they will fail at an inconvenient time if you ignore doing preventive maintenance).

Your RV repair shop will be happy to do all of these things for you for about $129 an hour. Even if it takes you twice as long to do some of these things, you're still making $65 an hour. That makes the work a lot more enjoyable.

Here Are Some Things You Can (and Should) Take Care of Regularly

- Clean the roof

- Check for leaks (I use a moisture meter)

- Re-caulk areas that look like they need it

- Check the tire pressure

- Check belts

- Inspect fluid levels

- Washing

- Waxing

- Check lights (Don't wait until you're ready to pull out of the driveway to find out that a brake light or turn signal is not working)

- Get a can of silicone spray and spray everything that moves. Then go back and do it again because I'm sure you missed some things—hinges and struts on the bay doors, steps, closet door hinges, slideouts, and leveling jacks. How about the gears under the bed for the slideout?

All of this sounds like a lot of work, but if you do a little bit every month, you can stay on top of things. You'll be amazed at the stress-free feeling you will get when you know all of these things are taken care of.

One last point: If you run into something that you don't understand or can't fix, get on the Internet and search the discussion forums for your type of rig and if you don't find an answer to your problem, ask a question.

In most cases, you will find a lot of fellow RVers willing to help you. Sometimes they will even point you to YouTube videos that will show you how to do what you were having a problem with.

RV Geeks is a great resource for this information. Here is a link to their videos on YouTube:

Youtube.com/results?q=RVGeeks

Bottom line: As I've said in a lot of other places in this book, it's a matter of attitude. Remember Tom Sawyer whitewashing the fence. With the right attitude, working on your RV can be fun and rewarding.

Look at your rig like a partner. You and your RV are going to tackle the world.

Chapter 4:

Hiking, Waterfalls, and Sunsets

"Any fool can criticize, condemn, and complain—and most fools do."

~*Benjamin Franklin*

If you want to relax, be stress-free, and enjoy RVing (and do this on a budget), you have to find something that you thoroughly enjoy doing, so you can have fun.

There's a difference between entertainment and fun. You have to make your own fun. If someone else tries to cause you to have fun, that's entertainment.

When I think of entertainment, I think about going to a concert or a ballgame or some event. These things can be entertaining, but I don't think of them as being relaxing or stress-free, and in most cases, they're sure not free.

Hiking

One of the best ways I've found to have fun and be relaxed and stress-free when I'm RVing is to do a lot of hiking. I know; hiking may not be your thing. You have to find your own joy, but if you haven't done much hiking lately, give it a try. You can start with short hikes, go at your own pace, and stop when you want to.

In every part of the country, there are interesting hiking trails. You can hike to lakes, rivers, rock formations, breathtaking views, beautiful forests, take a walk on the beach, and, of course, hike to waterfalls. The best part is just getting away from everything and being out in nature.

What Is the Difference Between Taking a Walk and Going Hiking?

We all more or less know the difference. You walk to the mailbox or you walk down the sidewalk, but you hike on a trail up to a waterfall.

Below are two definitions of hiking that I think do a good job of explaining what it is: Checking Google, the most common definition is as follows:

"To go on an extended walk for pleasure or exercise, especially in a natural setting."

I think that pretty well describes it.

If you're walking down the sidewalk in a city, you're getting good exercise, but that's not hiking in my mind. I don't know why—it's just not.

I think the Urban Dictionary explains why walking down a sidewalk is not hiking. Here is the way the Urban Dictionary defines hiking:

"Hiking is walking where it's ok to pee."

That definition works for me. Now that we know what hiking is, let's get on with talking about the joys of hiking.

Why I Like Hiking

- It's great exercise.

- You get to see things you can't see unless you hike— waterfalls, etc. (I know of three waterfalls that you can see from your car, though not very well: Multnomah Falls and Horsetail Falls in Oregon. And there's

Looking Glass Falls in NC. Even these three waterfalls can be seen and appreciated better if you get out of your car and walk a short distance to get closer to the falls. I know there are many other waterfalls that you can see without hiking, but these are my three favorites.

- It's free entertainment. I would rather go on a free hike than pay to go to a concert.

- Hiking clears your mind. You can do a lot of thinking while you're hiking.

- It's a great way to see and enjoy nature.

Unusual Hiking Trails

When I think of hiking, I think of being out in nature, but I've found some interesting hiking "trails" down the sidewalks in unique little towns. You can pick up the pace to get your heart rate up to whatever level you want.

Hiking and Exercise

Two of the best things about hiking are that it's great exercise and it's free entertainment. We could all use more exercise. When you're exercising you might think it's boring (and, for me, it is if I'm at a gym on a treadmill), but it's not boring when I'm hiking.

By the way, if you think exercise is boring, try living in a nursing home and see how boring that is. You might end up there sooner than you think if you don't get busy and exercise.

Some people say they can live without exercise. I'm sure they can but, in my opinion, they can't live as long.

Whether you're walking on the beach, hiking up a mountain trail or walking beside a pasture or wheat field, you'll find that it's great exercise, it clears your mind, and it's enjoyable. If you haven't been doing much hiking, give it a try and I think you will find it invigorating.

You can find interesting places to hike in every part of the country. Some of my most memorable hikes were when I was hiking in places that were not official trails. Hiking is a great way to see nature.

In a nutshell, hiking is great because your body does the same motion—walking—and you let the terrain determine how difficult it is. All you have to do is walk. The earth does the rest.

An added benefit of hiking: Researchers at the University of Michigan (in partnership with universities in England) have found that hikes in nature are linked with significantly lower stress levels and lower depression along with enhanced mental health and well-being. In other words, science has confirmed common sense.

Waterfalls

One word of caution. Rocks around waterfalls are slick and when you fall and land on them most of them are not very soft. In other words, be careful.

This past summer, I camped near a 120 foot high waterfall and almost every weekend I would hear sirens and see ambulances and rescue crews rushing by to go up the mountain and bring someone down on a stretcher. So be careful when hiking around waterfalls.

93 Years Old and Still Hiking to Waterfalls

Here is a picture of my mother hiking to a waterfall at age 93. She hiked the whole way there and back without stopping to rest. It was only a little over a half a mile, but it was a good hike.

She said seeing the waterfall was a wonderful reward at the end of the hike.

My mother at age 93 hiking to a waterfall

Waterfalls are Different

Some are cascading, some have water falling straight down, and of, course, many waterfalls are a combination.

Here is a picture of High Falls in DuPont State Recreational Forest, in North Carolina. It's one of my favorite waterfalls.

You have to hike a little over a mile up the mountain to get to the falls, but it's well worth the hike.

High Falls in DuPont State Recreational Forest

Sunsets

As the cover of the book shows, enjoying sunsets is one of the big advantages of the RVing adventure.

But if you're not taking the time to enjoy sunsets, you're missing what I consider to be one of the major benefits of RVing.

It's not just that sunsets are so beautiful and intriguing; the important thing is that, when you're watching a sunset, you can be totally relaxed. You're taking time for what's important in life.

It seems like there's no limit to the options for a sunset picture I could use here, but the one shown was taken on Christmas Day where I was camped in Cedar Key, FL.

Sunset in Cedar Key, Florida. To see it in color, go to www.LifeRV.com

Sunsets are more than a show of beautiful colors in the sky for 15 to 20 minutes. To me they symbolize freedom—freedom to just relax and be.

As Winnie the Pooh said, *"Sometimes I sits and thinks, and sometimes I just sits."*

I think maybe Winnie was thinking about looking at sunsets when he made that comment.

To me, relaxing and watching sunsets is just one of the many joys of RVing.

Bottom line: If you're RVing and not hiking and enjoying sunsets and waterfalls, you're missing out on what I consider to be some of the best parts of RVing life.

Hiking and enjoying sunsets and waterfalls is so much better (and less expensive—since it's free) than spending money on the things that tourists spend money on.

Chapter 5:

Local Music, Watering Holes, and Restaurants

"Go to Heaven for the climate, Hell for the company."

~ Mark Twain

One of the things I like about RVing adventures is getting to listen to local musicians play the local music of different areas.

There's Texas swing music played in the Bob Wells style, Cajun music (mainly in Louisiana), bluegrass (played almost everywhere), there's jazz in New Orleans, blues in

Memphis, Irish music, country music played everywhere, and the list goes on and on.

My favorite is old-time mountain music played mostly in the Southern Appalachian Mountains (but you can find pockets of it all over the country). That's why I spend a lot of time in the NC Mountains.

Live Local Music

I like almost all kinds of live music. There are a few exceptions. As my father said, "Rap music is about as close to music as Etch-A-Sketch is to art." Mark Twain said that classical music is not really as bad as it sounds—maybe some of it is, but most of it's OK.

Is a Fiddle Worth More Than a House?

I was talking to a woman last night at a local watering hole. We were talking about houses and music. She lives full time in her pop-up camper. She owns some land in NC and in VA. She travels back and forth between the two locations. She goes to Florida or somewhere warm in the winter months.

She loves to play old-time music (more about old-time music later). She can do that at a lot of jam sessions in the NC Mountains and in VA. She also likes to play

Cajun music, so she goes to Louisiana from time to time to do that (although there are starting to be more Cajun jam sessions in other parts of the country now).

Anyway, she was telling me that she'd just bought a new fiddle (new to her). She only paid $3,000 for her house (camper), and she paid more than that for her new fiddle.

It sounds like she has her priorities right when she pays more for her fiddle than for her house. By the way, if you've ever wondered what the difference is between a fiddle and a violin, the answer is simple. You're not likely to spill beer on a violin.

Are You Doing What You Love?

The point to all of this is that she is doing what she loves to do. You hear a lot of people saying that life is short. It's not that life is so short. It's just that death is so long.

Getting Back to Old-time Music

I didn't know there was a difference between bluegrass music and old-time music until I started spending a lot of time in the NC Mountains.

Below is a link to a video on YouTube showing some old-time music and flatfoot dancing. I shot this with my cell phone and didn't do any editing. Sorry about part of it being turned sideways.

Youtube.com/watch?v=xbhpqIh--fM

The musicians you see in the video at the above link are all playing for free. Well, they're not actually playing for free; they do get free beer while they're playing. It's not a band, just a jam session.

Maybe I shouldn't reveal one of my favorite places to listen to music when I'm in NC, but I will anyway. The video above was shot at *Jack of the Wood* in Asheville, NC. They have a Cajun jam session on Tuesday nights, old-time music on Wednesday nights, bluegrass on Thursday, and Irish music on Sunday afternoons and evenings.

There are places like this all over the country. Take the time to seek them out. You can't leave a place with live, local music and still feel stressed.

Jam Sessions Are Where You'll Hear True Local Music

I don't like concerts and shows where I have to pay to see the program. I like jam sessions in the local watering holes and other places around town that only the locals know about.

I like street musicians, too. Of course, some of them are good and some are just so-so.

Here is a link to a YouTube video of two street musicians playing in a park in Huntsville, AL.

https://www.youtube.com/watch?v=i4fVMF69YjQ

Here is a link to a YouTube video of a street musician playing in downtown Asheville, NC.

https://www.youtube.com/watch?v=jvOUSGwayho

One thing you will notice about street musicians is that they have to be different from regular musicians in order to attract a crowd.

In other words, whether you like their music or not, you have to say that they put on an unusual show.

Listening to jam sessions and street musicians is where you will hear the real local music and musicians. Most "shows" feature musicians from out of town. That's not my style.

Sometimes you will have to do some asking around to find out where and when the local jam session are, but, with enough asking, you can usually find good local music in almost every town. Do your homework and you will be well rewarded.

To find jam sessions ask around at music stores (the ones that sell musical instruments, not just places that sell CDs) and ask street musicians.

If you can find one musician who plays the kind of music you like, you can bet that he or she will know the inside information about where the local musicians hang out and have jam sessions playing that kind of music.

By the way, playing a musical instrument is one of the best ways I know of to eliminate stress. And almost any musical instrument can easily be carried in an RV.

One other thing, many RV parks now have jam sessions certain nights of the week.

The RV park where I'm staying now has bluegrass jams on Friday nights, country music jams on Saturday nights, and bluegrass gospel playing and singing for an hour on Sunday mornings.

Here is a link to one of the Sunday morning sessions. I shot this with my cell phone and didn't do any editing. As I pan around towards the water, you can see my white motorhome.

https://www.youtube.com/watch?v=5_9WUxtRwN4

Notice at about the one minute and 30 second point, you will see a woman play bluegrass gospel music on a cello.

Here is a video I shot of a musician playing at a local watering hole.

https://www.youtube.com/watch?v=1eHGdu1x3bY

I'll take this kind of music any day over a concert or a performance that I have to pay to attend.

When I look back and remember places I have been, one of the things that always comes to mind was what kind of music I heard there. To me that's one of the memorable parts of the area.

The kinds of music I like and have linked to may not be your kind of music, but do some asking around where you're camping and I'm sure you can find jam sessions playing the kind of music you like.

Make the effort and it will add a lot to your RV enjoyment. And one thing's for sure, it will eliminate stress.

Local Restaurants

Another thing I like to check out in new areas is the local food and atmosphere at mom and pop restaurants.

I don't order a burger or a pizza when I visit a new restaurant; I want to taste their specials.

One of the best ways to find these little unique places is to ask other campers who have been in the area for a while or ask some locals.

One thing I don't do is go to chain restaurants. An Olive Garden or an Outback is the same whether it's in Georgia or Arizona. I want to taste the local food.

Don't get me wrong. I like Olive Garden and Outback, but not when I'm looking for adventure and want to sample the local flavors.

For some people going to a strange restaurant and not knowing what to expect might be stressful, but to me that's part of the joy and adventure I'm seeking when I get in my RV.

I can't be disappointed because I don't go into local mom and pop restaurants with high expectations. I go in for the adventure. If the food turns out to be good (and it usually does) that's an added bonus.

Local Watering Holes

One of the best ways to get the flavor of an area is to visit one or more of the local watering holes (also known as pubs). Even if you don't drink, you can still go. They have non-alcoholic drinks.

A lot of times you can find live local music and even good local food at these places. The staff and usually most of the customers are locals, and they can tell you a lot about the area—where to find the best non-chain restaurants, where to find live music on which nights, and where to find other interesting watering holes and places to visit.

Bottom line: To add more fun to your RVing adventure and help eliminate stress, take in some local live music, try local food in some mom and pop restaurants, and check out the watering holes in the areas you visit. Sometimes you can get lucky and find all three of these things in one place.

Chapter 6

Find Time to Work on Hobbies and Projects

"Stop worrying about the potholes in the road and enjoy the journey."

~ Babs Hoffman

One of the best ways to be happy and stress-free is to have a hobby. There are a lot of hobbies that go well with the RVing lifestyle. It always amazes me to see the many hobbies people do.

A lot of people find that about the only time they have to enjoy their hobby or make progress on a project is when they get in their RV and hit the road for a while.

They find that it's a good time to get other distractions out of their lives.

If you don't have a hobby or something you really enjoy doing, consider taking up a hobby and taking it with you on your next RV adventure.

Here Are Just a Few Hobbies to Consider:

- Genealogy
- Painting
- Photography
- Writing
- Scrapbooking
- Fishing
- Golf
- Kayaking
- Jewelry making
- Crafts
- Ham Radio

- Computers

- Quilting

- Writing a blog

- Selling things on Amazon or eBay

I think you get the idea. When you have something you're looking forward to doing, the world looks brighter, and you don't usually experience any stress. You can't get bored when you have something to do that you're excited about doing.

Projects

In addition to hobbies, having a project to work on can do wonders for your attitude also.

I think the main difference between a project and a hobby is that a hobby is something you enjoy doing forever (or at least for a long period of time) whereas a project is something that has a beginning and an end.

For example, writing a book or designing a website would be considered a project.

It seems like I always have several projects going on.

I'm mainly talking about fun projects. I guess filing your income tax would be considered a project—not a fun project, but a project just the same.

I was talking to someone recently and I was just making casual conversation when I asked them what kind of projects they were working on. They didn't know what I was talking about. They said they didn't think they had any projects.

I couldn't imagine not having any projects.

I always have several projects going on. Learning to play a new song on the fiddle would be a project. I always have one or more songs I'm working on.

At one time my project was to learn to speak and understand Spanish. I spent six months living in Costa Rica, but I never did put enough effort into that project to get very good at it. Sooner or later, I'm going to start that project back up, but for now it's not a top priority.

You have to be careful not to have too many projects going on. That could be stressful in itself.

The easiest way to deal with too many projects is to just declare that something is no longer a project, at least for now—like me learning Spanish. I'm not behind on that project. I just declared that it wasn't a project for me right now.

For me, having free time to work on a project is like throwing Brer Rabbit in the briar patch. I couldn't be happier.

One of the main projects I usually have going on is writing another book. I sometimes feel a little let down when I finish a book. I like it when I'm working on a book.

I like to take a break between books—maybe a month or two. During that time, I can think about what my next book will be about, pick out a list of possible titles and subtitles, and consider some cover designs.

Unlike most other writers, I like to have at least a working version of a cover designed before I do much writing on a book. I may change it some (or even completely) before I finish the book, but I like to start with a cover design. It keeps me motivated.

Bottom line: To get the most enjoyment out of RVing, you cannot be bored or stressed out. You have to be looking forward to having time to yourself. One of the best ways to do this is to have a hobby and have some projects. Then having free time is like Brer Rabbit getting thrown into that briar patch.

Chapter 7:

Splurge and Save—the Right Mixture

"One of the funny things about the stock market is that every time one person buys, another sells, and both think they are astute."

~ William Feather

Whether they're going out for a weekend every now and then, using their RV for family vacations or even hitting the road full time, some RVers seem determined to do all of the tourist things.

They want to eat out all the time, drive as many miles as they can in a day, visit as many states as they can, and hit every attraction along the way.

The problem with trying to do RVing this way is that it soon gets stressful and it takes all the fun out of RVing. Another big problem is that if you RV this way you can plow through a lot of money pretty quickly.

Of course, if you take the approach that you're going to be extremely frugal and not spend money on much of anything except bare necessities, pretty soon you might realize that RVing is not much fun doing it that way either.

If you bought your RV so you could get away from it all, have fun, relax, get the hassles out of your life, and find some joy, just owning an RV won't make it happen.

One Important Key to Joy

There are several keys to joy, but one of the most important keys that I've discovered is that I can afford to do almost anything I want to—if I give up enough other things in order to stay within my budget.

In other words, I do the right mixture of splurging and saving to stay within my budget.

Look at it this way. You might think that there is this very nice (and expensive) restaurant that you would like to go to, but you have to settle and go to a much lower-price restaurant to stay within your budget.

You could go to the nice restaurant and then eat at home or go to McDonald's for as many meals as it takes to get you back within your budget.

This option might bring you a lot more joy than eating at the mediocre restaurant all the time.

Another example is that if there is a really expensive concert you want to attend, and you also want seats right up front, you could splurge and get the tickets you want, and then for your entertainment for the rest of the month (or longer if necessary) you could go hiking, watch sunsets, enjoy campfires, and basically do free stuff.

I think you will find that the splurge and save model will bring you a lot of joy.

One option that might bring you even more joy than splurging and then saving is to reverse things and save and then splurge. Just a thought.

A College Example

I remember when I was in college I calculated that it would cost me about $4 to go on a date (that was a long time ago). That would include two movie tickets, popcorn, maybe Cokes at a drive-in after the movie, and a little bit of gas. That sounds pretty reasonable until you realize I was washing dishes in the college cafeteria for 50 cents an hour.

(I was working my way through college because back then they didn't have student loans.)

The bottom line is that I would have to wash dishes for eight hours to get the money it would take to go on a date. I didn't date much in college because there were not many girls that I would wash dishes for eight hours to get to go out with—some of course, but not many.

I Bet It's Not a New Concept

This is probably not a new concept to you. There have probably been times when you saved all year to get to go on a two week vacation. You would do things and spend money on things while you were on vacation that you couldn't afford to do all the time, but with the right mixture of saving during the year and then splurging while you were on your vacation you found more joy than if you didn't save and didn't splurge.

Bottom line: Decide what things are important to you. Then think about what you're willing to give up to get to have or do those things. I think you will find a lot more joy in your RVing with the right mixture of splurging and saving.

Chapter 8:

Keep a Journal

"If at first you don't succeed—so much for skydiving."

~ Henny Youngman

Keeping a journal will help eliminate stress as much as anything I know.

Keep a journal as described in this chapter and it will take a load off of you and greatly reduce stress. Maybe not immediately, but as time goes on you will really start to appreciate all of the facts and information that have been recorded in your journal.

You will feel more organized and in control than you can imagine.

Nick Russell at <u>Gypsy Journal RV</u> recently posted the following comment on his site:

I can't tell you how many times people say, "We were someplace, I can't remember where it was now, but we had dinner in this great little restaurant, the name escapes me. But you really need to go try it out sometime."

I don't think I have ever been this bad when I'm talking to someone, but I've probably been pretty close.

Keep a journal and you won't have this problem.

Sometimes I can't remember where I had lunch yesterday, but I sure can't remember where I had lunch on June 3 last year.

A Journal Is Not a Diary with Your Innermost Thoughts

It's a chronological list of what happened in your life. Not everything of course, just the things and events that you think you might possibly want to know a year from now.

Here is a partial list of the kind of things and events that you should consider recording.

- What went wrong with your rig.

- What you did to fix the problem with your rig.

- What date you installed that new refrigerator.

- When you replaced that tire that blew out and how much you paid for it. (Of course, if you keep a maintenance log for your RV, you don't need to put this information in your journal. There's no need to list things in two places.)

- When you bought that new keyboard and how much you paid for it.

- The names of the camp hosts where you stayed when you were in AZ.

- The names of people and the names of their dogs you met at different campgrounds. Nothing impresses people and makes them feel like you really remember them than knowing their dog's name.

Basically, jot down anything you think you might possibly want to know a year from now.

Three to five minutes a day is all it will take, and you will be surprised how much you will use and appreciate this information. Of course, on some days there is nothing that happened that you want to write down.

There's no need to record events that are readily available elsewhere. For example, you don't have to record the date you bought something from Amazon. They keep that information for you. Just login to your Amazon account.

Bottom line: Have I convinced you to start keeping a journal yet? I hope so. It will save you a lot of frustration and add joy to your life.

Chapter 9:

Keeping Up with Routine Maintenance Will Eliminate a Lot of Stress

"If you could kick the person in the pants responsible for most of your trouble, you wouldn't sit for a month."

~ Theodore Roosevelt

Even better than keeping up with routine maintenance, stay ahead of it. Replace your brake pads before they're totally gone; replace belts and hoses before they break; replace wiper blades before they become totally useless.

One thing that is very important to an enjoyable and stress-free trip is to do a test run a few days before the big trip. This is especially important if your rig has been sitting unused for more than a month.

Check everything out and then crank it up and drive down the road for 10 minutes or so. This will also let you get the feel of driving it again. You can get rusty when you haven't driven (or towed) your RV for a few months.

A problem with not checking everything a few days ahead of time is that you could make unsafe decisions—for example, deciding to go ahead and leave when some things are not working, like a turn signal or a tire has low air pressure.

When the family is all loaded up and ready to leave and you find out that something is wrong, it's tempting to just go ahead and say that you will take care of it that night when you stop. That puts stress on you and could be dangerous, expensive or both.

Do your check-ride a week early, so you will have time to fix things before you leave. Knowing that everything is in good working order makes for an enjoyable RVing experience.

If You Want Smooth RVing, You Have to Oil Things

You probably didn't buy this book so I could tell you to oil things on your RV, but bear with me. I bet you will find things listed in this section that need to be oiled that you haven't thought of recently.

There is an old adage that says if it moves and it's not supposed to put duct tape on it and if it is supposed to move and it doesn't, put WD-40 on it.

I don't use much duct tape—maybe on a torn place on a wheel cover or on an awning, and I don't use much WD-40 (but it sure comes in handy when it is needed).

To prevent the need for the WD-40, I spray silicone lubricant on everything that moves, at least once a month. Start with all of the hinges inside and out.

You will probably remember to oil hinges, but make sure you get all of them. There are hinges on all of the cabinet doors inside the RV, but don't forget to spray the hinges on the outside storage bins. They take a beating with all of the rain and wind. And, of course, be sure to oil the hinges on the entrance door and the screen door.

Another thing you need to spray silicone oil on often is the struts (like the one shown below) that keep the overhead cabinet doors up when you open them. Don't forget the struts that are outside on the bay doors.

A Strut

Almost everything you buy for an RV is expensive, but here is one thing I found that was surprisingly inexpensive. You can get a pair of replacement struts from Amazon for $8 to $10 depending on the size and on which supplier you buy them from. Here's a link to ones I bought:

https://www.amazon.com/gp/product/B003VAT8KE

I had a hard time finding these because I forgot what they were called. They are struts just like the ones that hold the hood up on your car—except shorter, of course.

Here's a List of Some of the Things You Might Forget to Oil:

- TV antenna gears — This makes it so much easier to crank the antenna up and down.

- Steps — If you don't oil these frequently, they will start sticking and not go all the way in or all the way out.

- Leveling jacks — These are expensive to replace, so crawl under your RV and spray all sides of the shiny cylinder at least once a month.

- Slide gears — If you don't keep these oiled, they will stick or put a heavy load on your motor. Slide motors are expensive to replace.

- And, of course, grease the chassis when you change the oil.

- Handles on the storage bins.

- Entrance door latch and handle.

- Recliner — An occasional spray of silicone will keep it operating smoothly and quietly. Put a piece of cardboard under your recliner before you spray the silicone and leave it overnight so any excess oil won't end up on your carpet. Even if you have tile or hardwood floors, it's still a good idea to keep oil off of your floor.

- Driver's seat and the co-pilot's seat—including all of the cables and controls.

- I'm sure you will find other things that you can spray. Go for it.

Yes, I carry WD-40 with me, but I normally don't need it as long as I keep things moving freely in the first place by spraying everything regularly with silicone spray. And by spraying everything I don't have to listen to squeaks either.

A hobby is something you enjoy doing—golf, fishing, etc. For most people working on their RV doesn't fit into this category.

I heard a fellow RVer recently say, "I'm not very good with tools." My thought is that if you're going to own an RV, you better get good with tools. I don't mean you have to be an expert, but when you're paying an RV shop $129 an hour to do routine things, the bill (and the frustrations) can add up in a hurry.

One of the best ways to learn how to fix things on your RV is to hire a mobile RV tech when you have a problem that would normally require you to take your rig to an RV shop. One of the big advantages of using a mobile RV tech is that you get to watch what he's doing and you can ask questions.

In other words, you can learn a lot about your rig and how to fix things when you use a mobile RV tech. When you take your RV to a repair place, you don't get to go back in the shop and watch.

You can ask the mobile RV tech a lot of questions. Where is the water pump? How do I change the fuel filter for the generator? How do I change the engine air filter? There are some things that I take my motorhome to an RV shop to get repaired, but more and more I'm learning (and enjoying) doing a lot of things myself.

The mobile RV tech that I use doesn't work on the engine or chassis—just the RV. He doesn't do brakes, a grease job or change spark plugs.

An Example of Fixing It Yourself

Today I had a problem with my water pump. Maybe it wasn't a problem with the water pump. I could hear it making the pulsating sound when I flipped the switch, but I couldn't get any water when I wasn't connected to city water.

It had been working fine for three years. I had not checked it in almost a month, but I was planning on doing some boondocking—actually I'm planning on staying in a Walmart parking lot overnight in a few days—so I decided to check it. I'm glad I did.

I got the manual out and read what little it had to say about the water system, and then I decided to dig in and see what I could find out or fix.

Hoses behind the water manifold

As you can see in the above picture, when I took the six screws out of the water manifold and dropped it down so I could look at the pump, it looked like a rat's nest in there with all of the hoses. The good news was that I didn't see any leaks.

I disconnected what I thought was the hose on the output side of the pump, but it was the wrong one. I reconnected it, and disconnected the hose on the other side.

Then I went inside the RV and flipped the switch to turn the pump on. When I went back outside, water was gushing out of the pump. That was good news. It meant that the pump was working. I rushed back in and turned the pump off.

Then I connected the hose back to the pump, operated all of the valve handles and went back inside to check the system again and, low and behold, everything worked fine. I tried it a couple of times with city water connected and with it disconnected. I had water flowing just fine with the city water disconnected as long as I had the pump turned on.

I'm not sure what the problem was. I think it was that I didn't have the valve handles all the way in the correct position, but all that matters is that I now have it working, and I didn't have to pay an RV tech $129 or more—plus, now I know a lot more about how my water system works.

I'm not sure I can say that I enjoyed the process, but I'm glad that I know where my water pump is, how to get to it, and I know a little more about how my water system works.

I've found that when I stuff the white water hose back in the bay it can move the handles on some of the valves slightly and this can cause the system not to function properly.

Now if I have this problem again, before I take everything apart, I will move all of the valve handles and then make sure they are all in the correct position.

By the way, I found out that there is an asterisk stenciled on the water manifold plate showing the normal position of all of the valves. Now I know that. I'm getting smarter all the time. I'm glad I didn't pay an RV shop $129 an hour to fix that problem.

Things You Can Do to Your RV

- Are there any light bulbs that need replacing?

- Is changing to LEDs something that's on your list?

- Routine things like checking fluids and running the generator, replacing windshield wipers.

- Modifications? There's a never-ending list of things you can change or add to your RV—remote tire sensors, external tank sensors, a flat screen TV, a pure sine wave inverter, extra batteries, and the list goes on. These things cost money but save two hours of having your rig in the shop and that gives you $250 or so back in the budget to buy toys and gadgets.

- Oil or grease everything that moves.

- Check for water leaks in the roof. A moisture meter works wonders for this. Just check the moisture levels in the walls. Be sure to check in the corners.

- Check for water leaks everywhere you can get to water pipes—under the sink in the kitchen and bath room. Also check around the water manifold and the holding tanks.

- Clean out and organize your storage bins. Put everything in its place and throw away all of the junk.

- Check and clean your battery post and cable connections.

- Check the water level in your batteries and fill with distilled water if necessary.

- Sand and paint every place that looks rusty.

- While you're under the RV checking for rust, look for wires that are rubbing against something and not protected. A broken or shorted wire can be a hard problem to find. Tie wrap and tape loose wires and you can prevent some problems.

Keep your roof clean and keep an eye on all of the joints where a leak might develop. Use caulking and/or EternaBond tape to prevent leaks.

- And, of course, you can always do more waxing and polishing.

One Thing Not to Do

Don't put the stuff on your tires that makes them shine. Most of these contain petroleum products and these will cause the tires to dry out. Considering the price of tires, you sure don't want to do anything that will shorten their tires. Just keep the tires clean with soap and water.

One product that doesn't have any petroleum products in it and does provide good UV protection is <u>303 UV Marine Protectant</u>.

You can get it at Amazon at <u>Amazon.com/dp/B00JREJ9WU</u>

Take Advantage of Expert Information

RVs are made from a lot of parts from different manufacturers. When you have a problem with something—microwave, generator, toilet, backup camera or whatever—start by seeing if you have a manual and, if not, can you find a manual online? Consider calling tech support at the factory. Also, you can find YouTube videos showing how to do a lot of RV repair work.

Whether it's work or play depends mostly on your attitude. Take pride in having a well-maintained rig and the work will be a lot more enjoyable. RVs can last forever if you take care of them. I know people who have 50 and 60-year-old rigs that are in better condition (both mechanically and cosmetically) than most rigs on the road. Yours can be one of them.

I'm sure you've seen antique cars at car shows that are restored to mint condition. Your RV can be the same way if you take pride in it and take care of it.

Bottom line: Keeping up with routine and preventive maintenance will eliminate a lot of stress, and it can be an interesting and fun hobby. Give it a try. You might be surprised how much you enjoy it.

Chapter 10

Five Miscellaneous Ways to Reduce Stress and Increase Joy

"For my part, I travel not to go anywhere, but to go. I travel for travel's sake."

~ Robert Louis Stevenson

Just because I didn't devote a whole chapter to the issues below, don't consider them to be unimportant.

In fact, some of them are very important to your happiness.

- **Learn to drive and back your rig.** Being skilled at driving (and backing) your RV not only makes you safer, but it can add a lot of joy to your RVing experience.

When you're backing into a campsite with half a dozen people watching you and you haven't backed your rig since last year (or even if it was only last month), you're probably not going to get it right the first time—maybe not even on the fifth try. This situation takes some joy out of your RVing experience.

The best way to learn to drive your rig is to take a course with a certified instructor and let him teach you in your own RV.

One school that I would highly recommend is George Mayleben's RVSchool.com.

The next best thing is to go to RVBasicTraining.com and get their *RV Basic Training Manual*. Then get some cardboard boxes and go to a Walmart parking lot early on a Sunday morning when it's almost empty and practice turning, backing, etc. It's not as good as taking a course, but you can learn a lot this way. And if you run over a cardboard box, it's no big deal.

Remember, reading a book and practicing is not the same as actually taking an RV driving course; even if you get the book still make plans to take a driving course as soon as you can.

I'm an instrument rated pilot with over 2,000 hours of flying time, but I haven't flown much in several years. I remember reading an article in one of the flying magazines that said that doctors had the highest accident rate of any group of pilots. The reasons the article gave were that doctors didn't take enough time to do an adequate preflight check of the plane or the weather, they didn't fly enough to stay proficient, and they were overconfident. In other words, they had more confidence in their ability to fly than was justified. Make sure this doesn't describe you when you're driving or towing your RV.

In addition to the safety factor, imagine pulling into a campground and backing your rig (motorhome, fifth-wheel, or camper) perfectly into your camping space the first time—even with everyone watching. That in itself makes the cost of the driving course worthwhile.

One final point about what you'll learn by taking a driving course. Did you know that if you have a tire that blows out, you should mash the gas and not the brake? I know, hitting the brake would come natural, but that's the wrong thing to do. Take a driving course and find out why.

- **Kids need a space that's all their own for their stuff.** Of course, they need a place to sleep, but whether you're traveling full time, for a summer vacation or just for the weekend, kids need a space that's all their own. Not a big space, maybe just a drawer or even a laundry bag, but some place for their stuff that no one else will bother. Provide kids with their own space and you will have a bunch of happy campers.

- **Be patient with the other people traveling with you.** Pulling into a campground after a long day of driving when you're tired can be a frustrating time. There are a lot of little things to do, and you're mentally and physically tired. Remember that everyone else is too, so cut them some slack. Have patience with spouse, kids, and even your dog. Your dog may not be tired, but he is full of energy and wants to check things out and do something.

When I'm sitting in a campground and watching RVers pull in, I've overheard spouses talking to each other (and to the kids) in ways that I wouldn't talk to a dog—even if he had just crapped on the carpet.

Be patient and cut other people traveling with you some slack and you will have a much happier RVing experience.

- **Use a departure checklist.** In my early days of RVing there was one time when I had done everything I was supposed to and was ready to pull out. When I looked in my left side mirror, I could only see the side of my RV. I couldn't see behind it. I wondered how that mirror got knocked out of alignment. Then I realized that there was nothing wrong with the mirror. The problem was that I had not put the slide in. I was looking at the slide.

From that point on I used a checklist, and like Santa Claus, I check it twice. I should have known to use a checklist. All pilots religiously use a takeoff and a landing checklist. Having a checklist (and always using it) will make your RVing safer, less stressful, and more enjoyable.

Before I started using a checklist as I was pulling out of a campground or going down the road I would be wondering if I had remembered to do this or do that. That just adds more stress and takes away from the joy.

Checklists vary depending on the kind of rig you have, so make your own checklist and add to it from time to time as you realize that you have left some things off of your list.

- **Don't try to see, do or travel too much too fast.** It will all still be there next year. The most common mistake I see people who are new to RVing make is that they try to do too much too fast. It's hard to be relaxed when you're always rushed. Stop and smell the roses, take hikes, see the waterfalls, and sunsets.

Driving is fun, but if you do it all the time the new wears off of it and it becomes stressful, and it can get expensive.

Bottom line: RVing is a wonderful way of life whether you do it full time, use your RV for vacations or just for occasional weekend getaways. But sometimes it can get stressful and there will always be hassles to deal with. You can't eliminate all of the hassles and stress, but by following the advice in this book you can eliminate a lot of them.

The key to getting the most enjoyment out of your RVing is to learn how to deal with stress and hassle. In other words, your attitude is the most important factor.

Chapter 11:

Seven Things Every RVer Should Consider Owning

"In the end, it's not the years in your life that count. It's the life in your years."

~ *Abraham Lincoln*

As an engineer, I like gadgets, and there is seemingly an unlimited number of RVing gadgets available.

Some of these gadgets I consider to be extremely valuable, some are just nice to have.

Below is a list of the RVing gadgets that I think every RVer should consider owning.

Whether you should buy these gadgets or not will depend on your budget, and also on how much you use your RV.

If you only take a few trips a year or use your RV for a vacation or two, you may decide that it's better to take the risk than to spend the money.

But the more you use your RV the more you should seriously consider owning these devices.

1. A toolbox with a few tools. Even if you don't think you are good at fixing things, you should still consider having a toolbox with the following basic items:

A Phillips screwdriver, a flat head screwdriver, a pair of vice grips, a pair of needle nose plyers, a multimeter, a box of miscellaneous fuses, a roll of duct tape (or the new, stronger, Gorilla tape), a roll of black electrical tape, a can of silicone spray, and a few screws.

Having a toolbox stocked with these basic items will allow you to fix most minor things that break, stick, squeak, malfunction with your RV.

2. A GPS. A good GPS is extremely valuable. They make GPS models for RVers that have a lot information that is particularly useful to RVers, such as grades, overpass clearances, and location of dump stations.

I just have a regular GPS. It has a big 7" screen. I got it at a closeout sale and it was dirt cheap. If it ever dies, I plan to get one of the fancy ones with all of the RVing info on it.

In addition to having a good GPS, take the time to learn how to use all of the features. Usually even the low-priced GPS devices have more features than most people know how to use. Be the exception and master your GPS device.

One of my RVing proofreaders, Anna Edgren, provided the following information:

Your smartphone is also a reasonable substitute in many cases if you aren't splurging for the RVer specific GPS. Having a hands-free phone holder in the RV is key for this.

They also have driving apps that update with real-time info on road conditions, traffic backups, and speed traps. It is called Waze. You can download it at www.Waze.com. I had never heard of the app, but I downloaded it and started using it. I really like it. The price is right—it's free.

And, of course, always carry a good road atlas as a backup.

3. A tire pressure monitoring system. Tires are a major cause of stress or, at least, they should be.

But you can eliminate the stress associated with your tires with one simple (but not cheap) device.

One way to help make sure that all of your tires are properly inflated is to follow the conventional advice to check the tire pressure in all of your tires every morning before you hit the road, and then check them every time you stop for gas. Yeah, right. Who does that?

You hear a lot of horror stories about wrecks caused by tires blowing out. When you have a tire blowout, at the very least, you are out the cost of a new tire and many times a tire blowout causes damage to your RV even if you don't have a wreck.

In my opinion, a lot of tire blowouts are caused by a tire being underinflated, and gradually getting hot, or by the underinflated tire flexing the sidewalls until something gives.

The solution is to install a remote tire monitoring system that automatically monitors the pressure and temperature of each tire. It cycles through and gives you a digital readout of the temperature and pressure of each tire, and it sounds an alarm if any time any tire is over or under the pressure limits you have preset. It also monitors any sudden change in pressure. In other words, the system will alert you if a tire starts losing pressure rapidly even before the pressure gets too low.

There are several brands of tire monitoring systems on the market and the good news is I've never heard anything bad about any of them.

The only one I have first-hand knowledge about is the **Truck System Technologies model TST 507** system. You can find it at TSTtruck.com/product/tst-507sce-kit

I have used this system for three years and I have not had any problems with it.

Three other brands of tire-pressure monitoring systems (TPMS) that have received high ratings from RVers are:

- Tire Minder at www.MinderResearch.com

- Hawksnead Systems at www.tpms.ca

- Tire Tracker at www.TireTracker.com

There are a lot of gadgets that are nice to have, but a tire pressure monitoring system is one gadget that I think is absolutely essential.

Some people ask me if a tire pressure monitoring system is really necessary. To me it's like asking if collision insurance is really necessary.

You are risking your life and your pocketbook if you drive an RV without a tire pressure monitoring system.

I started out with a six-sensor system to monitor all six tires on my motorhome, but when I started towing my car, I added four more sensors to monitor the two tires on the dolly and the two tires on the back of the car. (The monitor will work with up to 10 sensors.) The system costs about $300, but as far as I'm concerned, it's just part of the cost of the RV.

Maybe if I had brand new tires, I might feel comfortable for a year of two without a tire monitoring system, but if I'm going to buy one sooner or later anyway, why not get it now? That's was my thinking.

Here's How to Own a Tire Pressure Monitoring Device for Free

If you think you can't afford a $300 tire pressure monitoring system, here's how to get one for free. Using round numbers, six tires at $400 each equals $2,400 for a set of new tires. Tires last five to seven years. Taking the seven-year maximum number, that means that tires cost you about $342 a year.

I figure that I will run my tires one year longer if I have a tire monitoring system, so by running my tires one extra year, I more than pay for the cost of the tire monitoring system. I guess you could say it's a matter of how you do your accounting.

How to Make Your Tires Last Longer

The three ways to make your tires last longer.

- Cover them and keep the sun's UV rays off of the tires when you're parked for more than a day or two.

- Drive your RV at least once a month. Tires have lubricants in the rubber that get released when the tire is being flexed. Driving your RV is also good for the engine and all moving parts. If you have a travel trailer or fifth-wheel, it's a little more trouble to hook things up and move it, but it will save on repair bills and make your tires and other things last longer. Of course, if you store your rig for the winter, driving it every month is not practical, but get it out as early as you can and drive it.

- Keep your tires properly inflated. Running a tire with low air pressure can damage a tire quickly.

As a backup plan, carry a good tire pressure gauge. I like the long type truck tire gauges.

I saw a guy this morning getting ready to pull out of the campground. He was doing the final walk around of his rig. He had a hammer and he hit each tire to make sure it had plenty of air in it. I don't know the last time he calibrated that hammer, but I want a more accurate test of my tire pressure.

One last point about tires: Know the age of your tires. Tires are good for five to seven years and time can slip up on you. After five to seven years, tires will start to dry rot and start to crack and become dangerous to drive on no matter how much tread is left.

Look for the 4-digit date code on the tires (sometimes it's on the inside under the RV). It's the last four digits in a series of numbers and letters that start with "DOT," as shown in the photo below. The first two digits are the week and the second two are the year the tire was manufactured. The tire in this photo was made in the third week of 2013.

This tire was made in the third week of 2013

One more point: As a backup, always carry a good tire pressure gage.

Bottom line about tires: Take care of your tires and you will have a lot less stress.

4. Get a good RV roadside service policy. RVs breakdown. Accept it. It's a fact of RVing life. Having someone come out and change a tire or finding someone who has the equipment to tow you to an RV service shop can be difficult and expensive. If you have a good RV roadside service policy, having a flat tire or breaking down beside the road is one less thing you will have to worry about.

Coach-Net and the Good Sam Club both offer good RV roadside service plans. With these plans they will come out and change a tire or tow you to an RV service center at no charge. I've never needed the service these companies offer, but for me it's peace of mind.

You can't expect to enjoy hassle-free RVing if you don't have one of these plans. The good news is that they are fairly inexpensive.

5. Know the height and weight of your rig. If you like the things that are on top of your RV and want to keep them (things like air conditioners and your TV antenna), here's the gadget you need. You need a little note stuck to your dash stating the height of your RV. Knowing that your rig is about 12 feet high won't cut it. Is it 12 feet and three inches or 11 feet and seven inches? Measure it and know for sure.

In order to get that little note, you first have to measure the height of your RV.

Here's the easy and accurate way to do it. Start by tying a string to the end of a plank. Then get someone to help you, and lay the plank on top of your air conditioner (or whatever is the highest part of your RV). Have the plank turned on edge so it won't sag. Then use a level to make sure the plank is level (don't eyeball it and say, "Yeah, that looks level.").

Have someone hold the string and mark it where it touches the ground. Then measure the length of the string from the ground to the bottom of the board, and you will know the height of your rig.

Of course, make sure your RV is on a level surface when you're doing this. Don't trust your memory. Write this measurement down and tape it to your dash. That little note will be a constant reminder to watch out when you're going under bridges, pulling into gas stations, etc.

You need to know the weight of your RV and not just the total weight. You need to know the weight of each wheel (or set of wheels if you have dual wheels).

You can have the four corners weighed at most RV rallies.

Be sure that your RV is fully loaded with people, supplies, and at least a half a tank of gas, propane, and water when you're getting it weighed. You will need to know this weight before you can know how much air pressure you need in your tires.

You can get the front and back weighed separately at many truck stops for $5 to $10. This beats nothing, but when you can you need to get all four corners weighed.

In most cases you will find that one side is a lot heaver then the other. By moving things around, you can get the weight closer to equal on both sides.

You need to inflate your tires on each axle to the same pressure and you need to inflate the tires to the recommended pressure for the heaviest side. You can't do this until you know the weight of all four corners.

6. Protect your electrical system. Campgrounds are notorious for having poor electrical systems. They have high voltage and low voltage conditions, and they sometimes have loose ground wires. In other words, from time to time campgrounds can have an electrical system that could damage your air conditioners, TVs, computers, and other electrical equipment. Not often, of course, but sometimes.

The best way to protect yourself from having a problem is to have a voltage monitoring and control system. They're not cheap ($300 to $400), and you may not need them often, but when you do need them, they're worth their weight in gold. On second thought, at the price of gold these days, maybe they're not that valuable.

There are different brands and different options, such as portable or hardwired, and you can get 30-amp or 50-amp versions.

I use Progressive Industries EMS-PT50C RV Electrical Management System. They have discontinued this model and have come out with the EMS-PT50X that has a better weatherproof shield over the receptacle.

Surge Guard is another company that makes a good line of electrical management devices.

All of these devices protect your RV from high voltage, low voltage, voltage surges, open ground, and voltage spikes. You can get versions that are just surge protectors that protect against voltage spikes. This is good protections, but not as good as a system that protects against spikes and also monitors and shuts power down when it detects a high or low voltage problem.

If you don't want to invest in an electrical management system right now, I would highly recommend that you at least get a plugin volt meter like the one shown below.

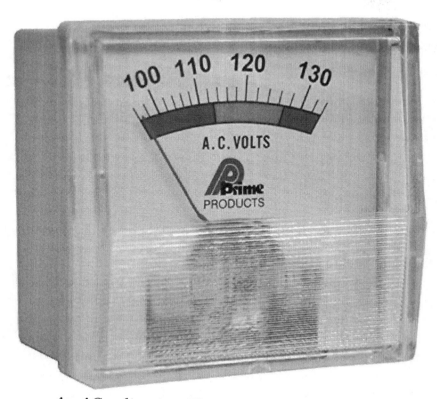

An AC voltmeter. Plug it into any AC outlet

You can get it from Amazon at the link below for about $17: https://www.amazon.com/dp/B002P48KLK

It has an adjustment screw on the front and you can calibrate it.

I found plugin digital meters for a lot less, but the one I ordered read three volts low (compared to an accurate digital multimeter) and there was no way to calibrate it.

One of the big reasons it would be a good idea to have a meter to monitor the 120 volt power is because, on a hot summer afternoon when everyone is running their air conditioner, the voltage can drop to a low level that could damage your air conditioner. Voltage below about 102 can damage an air conditioner.

7. Get some discount passes and memberships. Here are two that I would highly recommend.

Go to www.PassportAmerica.com and become a member of their Passport America program. You can join for $44 for a year, and you can camp at 1,900 campgrounds for 50% off. This will save you a lot of money if you camp often.

And if you are 62 or older, get a lifetime **National Parks Senior Pass** shown here.

National Parks Senior Pass

Right now it's $10, but on Dec. 10, 2016 Congress raised the price to $80, but they have not said when the price increase will go into effect. As of Feb., 2017 it hasn't gone up yet, but it will soon.

Here's where you can order the National Parks Senior Pass by mail:

https://store.usgs.gov/pass/senior_pass_application.pdf

At $80 it's still a great deal. It gives you and the passengers in your vehicle free admission to National Parks and Monuments, National Historic Sites, and discounts on camping at US Forest Service, Bureau of Land Management (BLM), and Corps of Engineers campgrounds. And remember, you buy this pass one time and it's good for the rest of your life.

There are other discount passes you can get that might be useful depending on how often you camp and where you like to camp.

Another one I like is www.HarvestHost.com. You can join for $44 a year and members can camp free at hundreds of farms and wineries. The way it works is that you are expected to buy some wine or fruit or vegetables while you're there. It sure beats parking overnight in a Walmart parking lot.

I have described several other discount programs in the *Other Resources* chapter. Check them out.

Other Miscellaneous Gadgets

The previous six things I consider absolutely necessary (or at least, extremely useful) if you want to RV worry and hassle-free. Of course, the more you travel and use your RV the more valuable and useful these things are.

First of all, let me point out one important thing to consider about the following gadgets.

Whether you should spend the money on these items can be decided based on two things: Your budget, and how much time you spend in your RV.

If your budget is tight, you can enjoy less hassle and more joy without any of these devices.

Also, if you use your RV mainly for a family vacation one or two weeks a year or if you use it for a few weekend getaways, you may decide not to invest in any of the following items.

In this section I just want to describe these things so you will know that they exist and when the need arises, you'll know what's available to solve the problem.

I have all of the things listed below and they are nice to have, but I could live without them. These are things you might want to consider putting on your Christmas and birthday wish list. Maybe somebody will buy them for you.

Here are some of the things I would put on this list:

A Clamp-on UHF Adapter for Your TV Antenna

The good news about this gadget is that your antenna may already have it.

Take a look at your TV antenna and if it doesn't have the little, short pieces shown in the picture below, you could greatly improve your UHF reception (channels 14 through 51) by adding the little booster antenna.

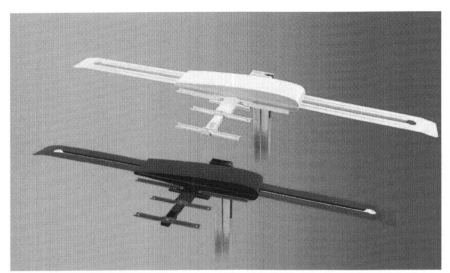

Winegard TV antenna with UHF booster attached

You can get the booster antenna for under $30 and it's easy to attach it to your existing antenna so your antenna will look like one of those in the picture.

The little booster antenna shown below is called a *Winegard RV-WING Wingman White UHF Booster TV Antenna.*

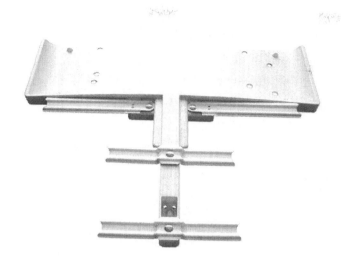

UHF booster antenna

Here is the link to the little booster antenna. The price was $27.53 the last time I checked.

Amazon.com/dpB001U2DPUE

For about $20 more you can replace the whole antenna head (everything except the pole). That's what I did. Here is the Amazon link to the complete antenna with that booster included.

www.amazon.com/dp/B003ZOH63W

Note that the black and white TV antennae shown previously are the same except for the color. Get one to match the color of your rig.

By the way, while you're up on the roof of your RV installing your UHF booster antenna, be sure to put a little grease or silicone spray on the gears that crank your antenna up and down. You'll be amazed at how much smoother it operates.

A Moisture Tester

These are especially useful when you're looking to buy an RV or trade for a different one. It's a quick and easy way to find out if the RV you're looking at has any leaks. Particularly check the four corners of the RV.

It's also a good idea to check your rig from time to time (especially after it's been raining for a few days). Caulking gets old and leaks develop.

You can get these meters on Amazon. Different models range in price from about $20 to $40. Here's the one I use. I got it from Amazon for $28.13.

www.amazon.com/dp/B00275F5O2

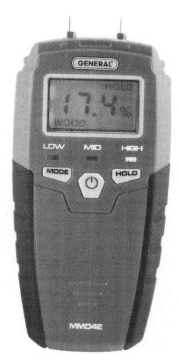

A Moisture Tester

An External Propane Tank and Hose Kit

The propane adapter kit consisting of a tee and a hose is used to allow motorhome owners to be able to hook their propane system to an auxiliary LP cylinder to avoid the need to move the motor coach to fill the propane supply when staying in one location for extended periods of time.

If you have a camper with external portable propane tanks, you won't need this kit, but it sure comes in handy if you have a motorhome with an internal propane tank and you want to stay in one place for longer than your propane tank will last.

One thing to keep in mind is that it's a good idea to crank your motorhome and drive it at least every month or so, therefore having to go get propane is not all bad. I do have the kit and I use it from time to time.

An added advantage is that the kit will allow you to operate your propane grill using your onboard propane.

The cost of an adapter kit (including the hose) will cost you about $53 on Amazon.

www.amazon.com/dp/B0014JKDB2

You can also get them at almost any RV store.

A Mr. Heater Portable Propane Heater

I try not to be where I need much heat, but even in parts of Florida a little heat feels good sometimes first thing in the morning.

I could use my propane furnace, but that heats the whole motorhome and uses a lot of propane.

I have a small electric heater that I use to heat up just the area where I'm sitting. I use this when the electricity is included in the price of my campsite, but if I'm paying for the electricity, heating with propane is less expensive, so I use my little Mr. Heater propane heater. These run to about $70 to $80 and are available at Walmart and on Amazon. You can find it on Amazon at this link.

www.amazon.com/dp/B002G51BZU

There is a smaller version for about $63 that is plenty big enough unless you're in really cold weather.

A Mr. Heater Buddy model propane heater

Of course, unless you're using your RV a lot and using it in cold weather, just take an electric heater from home and save the money—that is unless you're boondocking where you don't have access to electricity.

The key to this little heater being cheap to operate is to not always be buying new little green propane cylinders for $3 to $6 each. Buy a $10 adapter and refill the little tanks from your portable propane tank. This way the cost is about 60¢ to refill a cylinder.

Here's a link to a YouTube video that shows you how to do it.

Youtube.com/watch?v=LIeMDsj65Cs

You can also buy a hose that connects a larger propane tank to your heater.

In order not to damage your heater you will need a special hose or a filter sold by Mr. Heater when connecting the heater to a propane tank other than the little green cylinders.

A Pure Sine-wave Inverter

An inverter is a device to convert 12 volts DC to 120 VAC. They are useful (well, almost necessary) if you're boondocking.

You can get the cheap modified sine-wave inverters, and they work, but they put out voltage spikes that could damage computers, TVs and other electronic equipment. I've use a modified sine-wave inverter to run my TV and computer with no problem, but that doesn't mean I wouldn't someday have a problem if I continued using it.

If you're using a CPAP breathing machine, they specify that you should use a pure sine-wave inverter when you want to run them using a 12 volt battery. Keep in mind that, when running a CPAP breathing machine, if you run it without heating the water, it will use a lot less electricity.

The bottom line is that your electronic equipment is a lot safer and less likely to be damaged if you use a pure sine-wave inverter when you're boondocking.

One thing to keep in mind if you're buying one is to look at the specs—carefully. I bought one rated at 2,500 watts, which would run anything I wanted to run. When I got it, I found out that it had two 1,250 watt outlets. That wasn't what I was expecting.

Battery Voltage Meter

If you're boondocking, it's important to know what the voltage is on your house batteries. You can do a lot of damage to your batteries if you discharge them below about 12.0 volts (the 50% point) very many times.

So without a voltage meter connected to your batteries, you won't know when it's time to stop watching TV and go to bed (or else crank up your generator).

Also, there is no need to keep running your generator when your battery bank is fully charged.

They make high-priced solar controllers that monitor your battery voltage, and even tell you what percent of your battery you have left. If you boondock much, and have very many solar panels, you probably have one of these controllers already.

I have just one 100-watt portable Renogy solar panel. It allows me to run my computer, TV, LED lights, and charge my cell phone. It has a voltage meter on the little controller, but I have to go outside to see it.

I installed a $10 digital voltage meter right below my kitchen countertop and ran the wires back to my house battery bank. If you do this, be sure to put a fuse next to the battery in case the wires get pinched or shorted together.

If you use this meter to know the charge on your battery bank, take the time to read some articles and know what the numbers mean.

One thing to keep in mind is that when you're charging a battery, it's like filling a beer mug. You don't know how much beer is in the mug until the head has had time to settle.

The same is true about the battery voltage. You don't know what the real voltage is until the surface charge has dissipated, which will happen a few hours after you stop charging and the battery has been sitting and not being used.

A voltage of 12.7 with no load and the surface charge gone represents a fully charged lead-acid battery.

You can look at your battery voltage first thing in the morning before you start using it and know what percent charge you have on your battery.

Solar Panels

These are only useful if you plan to do any boondocking.

The Renogy 100 Watt Eclipse Monocrystalline Solar Suitcase with Charge Controller folds up like a suitcase and it has a handle. It's easy to store. As long as I have a reasonably sunny day, I can run my computer, charge my cell phone, keep a light on at night and watch TV for a little while with this little solar charger.

Renogy 100 Watt Solar Suitcase

It is a little expensive. I paid $299 a year ago when I bough mine. Now I see them priced at $399. Check, eBay, Amazon and the factory's website and hopefully, you can get a good price. *Renogy 100 watt Solar Suitcase*

Below is where I boondocked for two weeks at the Curtis Creek Campground in the Pisgah National Forest recently. This is near Old Fort, NC. You can see my little solar panel in the picture.

Boondocking for $2.50 a night using my solar panel

The regular price for camping there is $5 a night, but with my *Senior Pass*, it only costs me $2.50 a night. I more than saved enough on camping fees during the 14 days to pay for my solar panel.

There was no electricity at the campground, but with my little solar panel, I did just fine.

On average I get about twice as much power from this suitcase solar panel as I would get from one mounted on top of the RV because it's not laying flat and also, I can keep it pointed towards the sun.

If you want to relax and get away from it all, do some boondocking and you will know the meaning of relaxed RVing.

By the way, there was a well stocked trout stream right behind my motorhome.

Some of these things you may already have, and some of them would not be of use to you if you don't boondock.

And, of course, some of the gadgets might be nice to have but you wouldn't use them enough to justify the price.

Of course, I didn't begin to cover all of the gadgets you can get for your rig. For almost any problem you can think of, there is a gadget that will solve your problem— or at least claim to. If you're a gadget freak like me, buying gadgets could get expensive.

Bottom line: Don't get carried away with buying all of these gadgets right away. I just wanted you to know about them, so you could get the ones that would really make your RVing less stressful and more enjoyable.

Chapter 12

If You Can't Laugh at Yourself, Let Me Know and I'll Laugh at You

"Everything is funny, as long as it's happening to somebody else."

~ Will Rogers

You have probably noticed a constant theme throughout this book: To really enjoy RVing, you have to find ways to eliminate as much stress as possible.

There are a lot of things that cause stress, but by making some small changes you can eliminate much of it.

I've talked about several of those in the book so far.

One of the biggest things you can do to help eliminate stress is adjust your attitude. There are going to be things that will go wrong when you're RVing. We have talked about several of these things and what you can do to prevent the problems, but you can never prevent all stressful situations.

The most important thing you can do is learn to let stressful situations roll off like water off of a duck's back. I know that's easier said than done.

Have a Sense of Humor

One thing that helps a lot is to have a sense of humor. A lot of things are funny the week or month after they happen, but not so much immediately. And, of course, as Will Rogers said, things are funnier when they happen to someone else.

I remember one woman telling about the time she was all dressed up in a fancy dress and high heels waiting for her husband to get home. They were going out to dinner with another couple at a fancy restaurant.

Her husband would need to take a shower when he got home and he was running late, and the gray water tank was almost full, so the woman decided that she would go ahead and drain the tanks.

Everything was already hooked up. All she had to do was pull the black water tank handle, let it drain and then close it, and do the same thing with the gray water tank.

She went outside, opened the bay door and, straddled the sewer hose. Then she pulled the handle to drain the the black water tank.

That's When the "Ship Hit the Sand"

To make a long story short, sometime over the last few days, raccoons or opossums had been out there and their sharp claws had put dozens of little holes in the sewer hose. Raw sewage sprayed all over the woman like it was coming out of a sprinkler hose before she could get the valve closed. She was soaked in raw sewage from head to toe.

If that had happened to you, could you laugh? It would probably be easier to laugh later on when you were telling it, and of course, it would be real easy to laugh if it had happened to someone else. You're probably laughing now just thinking about the situation and picturing it in your mind.

When something happens that tends to stress you out, think about this story. Whatever you're finding stressful, it's probably not this bad. Just ask yourself if you would rather be in your present situation or in her situation.

This lady was laughing about the event when she was telling me the story, but that was a month or so after it happened. I doubt if she was laughing at the time.

Another True Story

Last night, I was talking to a woman who had just taken an old motorhome from Florida to California and back. She said, "I think it broke down in every state. When the first tow truck was towing me and I was sitting in the passenger's seat riding along, I had a great view and he was doing the driving. It was nice."

She said, "I should have asked him how much he would charge to tow me to California and back. It would have probably been cheaper than what I spent on the trip with all of the breakdowns."

I doubt if she was laughing each time she broke down, but last night sitting around a campfire telling the story she (along with everyone else) thought it was pretty funny.

To have less hassle and more joy in your RVing life, you have to learn to laugh at situations and not let them stress you out.

Not everything is a laughing matter, but try not to get stressed out about things. Deal with problems, and find the humor in the situation when you can.

Bottom line: Remember, if you can't laugh at yourself, let me know and I'll laugh at you.

Chapter 13:

Closing Comments

"Wine is constant proof that God loves us and loves to see us happy."

~ *Benjamin Franklin*

After reading this far, you're armed with the knowledge and skills to enjoy RVing with less hassle and more joy (just as the title of the book promised).

In a nutshell, the secret to having a happy, hassle-free, and stress-free RV adventure comes down to first using the techniques, gadgets, and hacks described in this book to eliminate most of the hassles that cause you stress.

Then all you have to do is use the techniques I've explained in this book to deal with the stressful things and events that you can't change.

The Most Important Thing

Of course, the most important point is to adjust your attitude. Attitude is more important than anything else when it comes to having a hassle-free, and stress-free RVing adventure.

Refer back to the different chapters of the book as you need to and remember. . .

Don't sweat the small stuff and it's all small stuff.

Well, most of it is small stuff. Having a major mechanical breakdown or having a refrigerator go out is a slightly bigger issue. But not really, it just means you have to write a bigger check out of your emergency fund.

Surprisingly, it's not the big things that seem to stress people out and take the joy out of RVing—it's the little things.

One of the main reasons you wanted an RV in the first place was so you could get away from it all and enjoy some relaxed, adventuresome, stress-free living. Now you know how to make that happen.

Since you're reading this book, I assume you already have an RV and have some experience living part of the time in it.

Now that you know how to make it a stress-free adventure, you may be thinking about whether it's possible and feasible to live full time in your RV.

What about Living Full Time in Your RV?

I have lived full time in my motorhome for four years now and I wouldn't want to live any other way. The fulltime lifestyle is not for everyone. In fact, I don't even think it's the right lifestyle for most people.

It's a lifestyle for people who are looking for adventure, freedom, and a stress-free, relaxing life.

If you're thinking you want to look further into the idea of living full time in a RV, I have written five other books covering the topic for different groups of people.

The book *Home no Longer Has to be a Place* will help you decide if you really want to live full time in an RV. I'm thinking about changing the title of this book from "a Place" to "one Place."

The *Young RVers* book is for people who are not retired and need to still be working and making a living while they're RVing.

The *Secrets of RVing on Social Security* explains how it's possible to live the RVing lifestyle on a frugal budget. A lot of people are doing it and having the time of their lives. If you do it right, it doesn't take a lot of money to live the full-time RV lifestyle.

My most popular book is *Motorhome and RV Retirement Living*.

You don't need all of these books. In fact, part of the information and some topics are covered in more than one book. If you want to pursue the idea of living full-time in an RV, pick out the book that fits your situation and you will find a lot of information to help you make your decision and show you how to make it happen.

One other point: To live fulltime in an RV you will have to get rid of a lot of stuff. If you need help doing this, my book *Tidying Up—The Magic and Secrets of Decluttering Your Home and Your Life* will show you how to do it the easy way.

I don't mean to be pushing my other books (oh wait, yes I do).

Anyway, take a look at my other books and if any of them appeal to you, they're available on Amazon.

When you learn to live the RVing adventure stress-free, you may find yourself singing the song from the Disney movie *Song of the South*. It goes like this:

Zip-A-Dee-Doo-Dah
Zip-A-Dee-A

My oh my, what a wonderful day

Plenty of sunshine heading my way

Zip-A-Dee-Doo-Dah
Zip-A-Dee-A

If you have questions for me, feel free to email me at Jminchey@gmail.com.

If you found this book helpful, please go to Amazon and leave a review.

Reviews are greatly appreciated.

Chapter 14:

Other Resources

"If you want a guarantee, buy a toaster."

~ Clint Eastwood

This chapter contains information on resources that I think you will find helpful. Many of these links and resources have been pointed out previously in different parts of the book, but I'm including them here so you will have what I consider to be the most useful references all in one place.

I have placed the links in categories. Some of the links could fit in more than one category, but I tried to put them in the category that they best fit in. You will find a few of the links listed in more than one category. I did this in order to make the categories more comprehensive.

Most of the people I link to in this chapter are full-time RVers. I know that you're probably not living full-time in your RV like these people, but the information is still just as valid whether you're a full-time, part-time or sometime RVer.

Blogs I Follow

Technomadia.com – Cherie and Chris have been full-time RVing for over 10 years. They say a technomadia is a technology enabled nomad. That's where the name of their website came from. They travel in a very fancy converted bus, that they have geeked-out. Their site is a wealth of information for all aspects of RVing and especially for anything to do with technology or traveling. They have written a great book, *The Mobile Internet Handbook*, which is the bible when it comes to getting connected to the Internet while on the road. You can find this book (and their other books and apps) on their website and on Amazon.

Wheelingit.us – Nina and Paul Wheeling travel in a 40 foot Class A motorhome. Nina writes one of the most information-rich blogs on the Internet. They do a lot of boondocking and she writes some wonderful blog-posts on boondocking as well as traveling and other RVing subjects.

GoneWithTheWynns.net – Nikki and Jason Wynn sold everything, bought an RV and off they went to discover the world—at least the part they could get to in their motorhome. They provide a lot of great articles and entertaining, high-quality videos that cover their travels, equipment, and all aspects of RVing. (Update as of Jan. 2017): Now they have sold their motorhome and bought a catamaran sailboat and are living full time on their sailboat sailing around the Caribbean. They are adding a lot of articles and videos now about sailing, but the vast archives of RVing articles and videos on their website are well worth looking at. Reading their blog is fun, enjoyable, and informative. You'll love it.

InterstellarOrchard.com – Becky Schade is in her mid-30s, college educated, and a single female RVer who has been living full time in her 17-foot Casita camper for over four years. She lives on a very tight budget and pays for her lifestyle by doing workamping at Amazon, working at National Parks, and sometimes she does other gigs. She also supplements her income by writing. Her book, *Solo*

Full-time RVing on a Budget – Go Small, Go Now, is a great book if you're on a tight budget and looking to get started RVing. You can find the book on her website, and on Amazon. When you visit her website be sure to click on the link to "Useful Stuff" in the top navigation, bar. It really is useful stuff. She has a new book out now, *The Little Guide to Dreaming BIG*. If you have a dream, but it's not just the ordinary, everyday kind of dream, it's an unrealistic, crazy sort of dream that makes your heart sing, and brings a little light into the dull routine of your day, this book is for you.

CheapRVLiving.com – Bob Wells has been living in a van for 15 years. He boondocks most of the time and lives mainly from his Social Security income plus income from writing and occasionally he does some workamping jobs as a camp host. In addition to explaining how he lives, he also writes some great blog posts (that include wonderful pictures) about his travels and where he's camping.

GypsyJournalRV.com/category/nicksblog – Nick Russell and his wife Terry have been RVing full time for 17 years. Nick has written 25 books and he writes a blog post about RVing every day. He also writes a monthly publication called the *Gypsy Journal*. You can learn more about it at: GypsyJournalRV.com. (Update as of Jan. 2017): Nick has bought a house in Florida and will be staying there during the winter months and RVing the rest of the year.

FloridaOutdoorsRV.com/pages/top-rv-blogs – You can learn a lot from blogs and if you want to follow even more blogs than the ones I've listed here, this link will take you to a list of what is called the "**Top 50 RV Blogs.**" It also provides a brief description of each one. I don't follow all 50 of these blogs, if I did I wouldn't have time to do anything else, but take a look at the list and see if any of them look interesting to you. My guess is you'll find some you like.

RV Forums

Reading forums is a great way to learn about RVing. You can see what questions other RVers are asking (and see the answers being posted by fellow RVers). You can also get answers to your own questions. Here are the three popular RV forums I follow almost every day.

RV.net/forum – Note that this website has a dot **net** and not a dot **com** suffix. The discussion group is broken into several categories—Class A, Fifth-wheels, Workamping, etc. Check out the different discussion groups and you will learn a lot. I check into these forums almost daily.

RV-dreams.activeboard.com – This is an active discussion forum with the discussions sorted by topics. Check out the *Community Chat* section, the *Buying an RV*, and the *RV Maintenance* sections or others that look interesting to you.

iRV2.com/forums – This is another active RVing forum that I check frequently.

Other RVing Forums – In addition to the popular forums listed above, there are forums for just about every brand and type of RV (Roadtrek, Airstream, National, Casita, Fleetwood, Forest River, Tiffin, etc.). Search Google and find the forum for your rig. It will be a great place to get answers to the many questions you will have about your RV. For example, "Where is the fuse for the water pump?" Your manual may not tell you, but someone on the forum for your type of RV will know, and tell you almost immediately.

Finding Campgrounds

Sometimes I pay full price for a campsite, but most of the time I get discounts of up to 50%. There are two main ways I get the 50% discounts. First, I can almost always get discounts of 50% or more by booking a campsite for a month at a time. That's what I usually do. The second way I get the 50% discounts is by using one of the websites or apps below:

PassportAmerica.com – Membership is $44 a year and you get a 50% discount at 1,900 campgrounds all around the country. Stay two or three nights and you've paid for your whole year's membership. I consider being a member of Passport America one of the best investments in the RV world.

AllStays.com – This site has a lot of campground and travel information. You can also get their information as an app for your iPhone, iPad, iPod or Android device at **AllStays.com/app**

RVparking.com – This site has reviews and recommendations for 19,000 campgrounds. One thing I like about this site is that you get to see why people like or dislike a particular campground.

OvernightRVparking.com – Membership is $24.95 a year. They have the web's largest database of free RV parking locations in the US and Canada. Their database contains 12,783 RV Parking and No Parking locations in the USA and Canada. Search by your current location, city and state or province or zip code. Download PDF files by state or province.

UltimateCampgrounds.com – This site provides comprehensive information about 28,000 public campgrounds of all types in the US and Canada. They also have an app.

DaysEndDirectory.com – This site provides information about free and low-cost RV parking. To get access to this information you have to be a member of Escapees.com. Having access to this site is one of the many benefits of joining Escapees.com.

America the Beautiful Senior Pass – If you're 62 or older and are a US citizen, you can purchase the *America the Beautiful National Parks and Federal Recreational Lands Pass*. It's also called the *Senior Pass*. It's $10 for a lifetime membership if you buy it in person or $20 if you want to receive it by mail. It allows you free admission and discount camping (which is usually a 50% discount). In Dec., 2017, Congress passed a law raising the price to $80, but as of Jan. 2017 it has not gone into effect. There is no published date when the price increase will go into effect. Even at the new $80 price, it's a real bargain.

You can get the pass by mail by going to this website: **store.usgs.gov/pass/senior.html** and to find locations where you can get the pass in person, go to:

store.usgs.gov/pass/PassIssuanceList.pdf

I recently visited Curtis Creek campground in the Pisgah National Forest in North Carolina. There were 14 campsites there and only two of them were occupied. With the pass the cost was only $2.50 a night to camp and enjoy some of the most beautiful views in the North Carolina Mountains. You have to go about three miles up the mountain on a gravel road, but there is no problem getting a Class A motorhome to the campground.

FreeCampsites.net – This is a free website that allows you to search for free camping places. You can enter a city and state or a zip code and see a map showing free camping places. In most cases there is information about each site in addition to its location.

HarvestHosts.com – This is a great resource for finding farms and wineries all over the country where you can camp overnight for free. Staying overnight at a winery or farm is a fun experience. Membership is $44 a year. I find it well worth the membership fee. Harvest Hosts provides you the opportunity to travel to new areas, have unique experiences and enjoy purchasing locally grown and produced products. (You are expected to buy a bottle or two of wine or some fruits or vegetables.)

CasinoCamper.net – Most casinos will allow you to camp overnight and many of them will even give you some free chips (they want to get you inside so you will start gambling). If your luck is like mine, this option might end up costing you more than just camping at an RV park.

Walmart.com – Most people don't think of Walmart as an RV park, but most Walmart stores allow RVers free overnight parking. Last week I spent the night in a Walmart parking lot and there were about 40 other RVs there. They started coming in about 5:00 p.m. and most of them were gone by 8:00 the next morning. Be sure to call or check with the manager to get permission. In some locations city or county ordinances make it illegal to park overnight in the Walmart parking lots.

BoondockersWelcome.com – This website lists hundreds of places where you can boondock free of charge. You will generally be camping in other RVers driveways. It's $24.95 a year if you will only be a guest, and $19.95 if you have a place and agree to also let RVers camp free in your driveway.

If you agree to be a host and let people boondock in your driveway, they don't just show up. They contact you and get permission. You only let people boondock at your place when it's convenient for you. If you're going to be out of town or having company, you probably don't want boondockers during that time.

I haven't used this website yet, but everyone I've talked to who has used it said they had a wonderful experience when they did. The hosts are friendly, gracious and happy to have you. They like to have fellow RVers to talk and visit with.

RVing Videos I Like

Search YouTube for the word "RV" and you will find 3.5 million videos. Some are extremely useful and informative, some have bad and untrue information. Some are interesting and entertaining, and some are just plain boring.

I haven't watched all 3.5 million of the videos, but I have watched a lot of them (and I do mean a lot). Below are the ones I consider to be worth your time to watch. Turn off the TV and spend an hour or so watching these videos and you will be entertained and informed.

- **Youtube.com/watch?v=a3MvhrkbWb8ube.com/watch ?v=a3MvhrkbWb8** – Shirley Walker is 73 and she travels around the country and lives full time in her Class C motorhome. If you're wondering whether she's enjoying her life or not, watch this 7-minute YouTube video and decide for yourself. To me, this video is inspiring for us old folks. You can skip some of the links to articles and videos I provide in this book and not miss anything really important, but I highly recommend that you stop and watch this video.

- **Vimeo.com/71385845** – I love this 7-minute video. It's about a young couple and their full-time RVing adventure traveling with a small child. Take a look at it. I think you'll like it.

- **YouTube.com/watch?v=NGxmSGf2Kr8** – This 14-minute video shows 17 full-time RVers as they describe how they make a living while living the RVing lifestyle. If you're looking to make some extra money while you enjoy RVing, maybe you can get some ideas from these RVers.

- **Youtube.com/watch?v=g0UJAMNXJbk** – This 8-minute video is an interview with a retired couple describing their life on the road and how and why they decided to make the transition to the full-time RVing lifestyle.

- **Youtube.com/watch?v=jAhBnq2pLNk** – This is another 8-minute video interview with a retired couple.

- **YouTube.com/watch?v=ebbo800_Rg0** – This 11-minute video interview is with a young, single, female RVer. If you're thinking about being a solo RVer, I think you will find her story interesting. By the way, she has now been on the road for 4+ years and is still loving the lifestyle.

- **Youtube.com/results?search_query=rvgeeks**

  This is a link to a list of how-to RV videos by RV Geeks. You will find a lot of useful information in these videos.

- **TechNomadia.com/ramblings** – If you like the interview style of the previous videos, this link will take you to dozens of these videos produced by Chris and Cherie at . **TechNomadia.com**

RVing Books I Like

With most eBooks priced at $2.99, you can get a lot of RVing information for very little money. Here are some of my favorite RVing books.

Buying a Used Motorhome – How to get the most for your money and not get burned, by Bill Myers. Don't even think about buying a motorhome without reading this book. The information in this book saved me thousands of dollars. And, even more importantly, it helped me pick the right motorhome for my needs and budget. The book is about buying a used motorhome, but a lot of the information would be useful and helpful if you were considering buying a travel trailer or fifth-wheel camper. You can find the book on Amazon at this link: **Amazon.com/dp/14793653**

Solo Full-time RVing on a Budget – Go Small, Go Now, *by* Becky Schade. You can find the book on Amazon at this link: **Amazon.com/dp/B00W30OFCE**

Or you can find it on her website at **InterstellarOrchard.com**.

She has another book *The little Guide to Dreaming BIG*. You can find it at this link: **Amazon.com/dp/B01HREJMZK**

The Mobile Internet Handbook: 2016 US RVers Edition – This comprehensive guide to mobile internet options for US based RVers was written by full-time RVing technomads Chris and Cherie of **Technomadia.com**. You can get the book on Amazon at this link: **Amazon.com/dp/1530237505**

Convert Your Minivan into a Mini RV Camper, by William H. Myers. For $200 to $300 and a minivan, you can have an RV that you can comfortably live in. You can find the book on Amazon at this link: **Amazon.com/dp/1530265126**

How to Live In a Car, Van, or RV: And Get Out of Debt, Travel, and Find True Freedom, by Bob Wells. You can find the book on Amazon at this link: **Amazon.com/dp/1479215899**

RV Basic Training Manual – Motorhome Driving Course. Learn what every commercial driver MUST know and ever RV driver SHOULD know. The book is a little pricy at $30, but well worth it. It's a 46-page manual with a lot of pictures and drawings, so it's easy to read. You can order it at this website:

RvBasicTraining.com/buy-manual.html

Get What's Yours – The secrets to Maxing Out Your Social Security, by Laurence J. Kotlikoff and Philip Moeller. You can get the book from Amazon at:

Amazon.com/dp/B00LD1OPP6

Motorhome and RV Retirement – The Most Enjoyable and Least Expensive Way to Retire by Jerry Minchey. (This is one of my books so, of course, I think it's a good book.) Note that some of the basic information in that book is the same as what's in the book you're reading, but a lot of the information in that book is not in this book. You can find the book on Amazon at this link:

Amazon.com/dp/098449684X

RVing Novels: If you're looking for some great novels with plots built around RVing, I would recommend the Mango Bob series. The series includes *Mango Bob, Mango Lucky, Mango Bay, Mango Glades, Mango Key* and *Mango Blues*. They all revolve around a 35-year-old single guy and his adventures as he lives and travels around Florida in his motorhome. I have read all of the books in this series and love them. You can find them on Amazon at this link: **Amazon.com/dp/1889562033**

RVing Groups

Escapees.com – I recommend joining this group. It's $39.95 a year and you also get membership in the new **Xscapers.com** group (which is for younger RVers) at no extra charge. With your membership you will receive their printed magazine every other month. I consider this the most useful RVing magazine in the industry. They also offer discounts on insurance, camping, and a lot of other things I spend money on. Take a look at their website and see if you think what they offer would be useful to you.

RVillage.com – This is a free website and it's a great way to keep up with where your RVing friends are and let them know where you are.

FMCA.com – The Family Motorhome Association is a popular group of RVers that has been around for a long time. Take a look at their website and the benefits they offer. The cost is $50 for the first year and $40 for renewals. One of the things they offer is a program for getting great discounts on Michelin tires. They also host awesome RVing rallies. There were over 3,000 RVs at one of their recent rallies.

Healthcare on the Road Is Changing

Important note: As of Jan. 20, 2017 your healthcare options will be changing (and will probably continue to change for the next year or so).

Be sure to check these six websites to get the latest information.

Here are six websites that will give you the latest information about getting healthcare when you're a full-time RVer.

- RVerInsurance.com

- RverHIExchange.com

- TheHealthSherpa.com

- Teladoc.com – 24/7 access to a doctor, by phone.

- 24-7HealthInsurance.com

- Kff.org/interactive/subsidy-calculator – This is a link to a website that has a handy tool to provide estimates of health insurance premiums and subsidies for people purchasing insurance on their own in health insurance exchanges created by the ACA (Affordable Care Act). It will most likely be updated to include information on new programs that become available. Check it out.

How to Find Work as an RVer

If you're RVing full time or thinking about it and want to do some part-time work while you're RVing, the websites below will be useful to you.

CoolWorks.com – This is a free site.

CoolWorks.com/jobs-with-rv-spaces – This link goes directly to a page on the above website that probably has what you're looking for.

Workamper.com – This is a subscription website. The cost is $27 a year.

Work-for-RVers-and-Campers.com

Apps

AllStays.com/apps/camprv.htm – This is the app I use the most. With this app I can find reviews on almost 30,000 campgrounds, find locations of dump stations, find overhead clearances, and even find grades on steep mountain roads. It costs $9.99 to download the app to your iPhone or Android device.

RVParking.com – This app contains almost a quarter of a million reviews about 20,000 campgrounds. The price is right for this app—it's free.

US Public Lands – About 30% of the land in the US is owned by the government. If you've ever wanted to know where to camp free on government land, you'll love this app. This app shows BLM, Forest Service, NPS and public land boundary maps. You can download the app from Google Play or iTunes.

Reserve.WanderingLabs.com – When you check for availability at a campground and there's no campsite available on the dates you want to camp, instead of checking back every few days, let this app do it for you. Instead of checking back every few days it will check every few minutes and send you an email as soon as a space becomes available.

The app is free, but if you want to make a small donation, you can get the version that checks constantly instead of every few minutes.

Waze.com – Your smartphone can be a reasonable substitute for an RVer specific GPS. By RVer specific GPS, I mean one that gives you information about bridge clearances, grades, dump stations, etc.

Having a hands-free phone holder in the RV is key for this.

This app also has real-time info on road conditions, traffic backups, and speed traps. It's called Waze. You can download it at www.Waze.com. I really like it. The price is right too—it's free.

Other Websites

Spend an evening or two reading the articles and watching the videos you'll find on the websites listed below and you'll know more about RVing than 90% of the RVers out there. Best of all, I think you'll find the way the information is presented in these videos to be enjoyable and entertaining.

I check these websites for new information at least once a week. Most of them have a way to sign up and get an email message when new information is posted.

Technomadia.com – Chris and Cherie have been full-time RVers for more than 10 years. They share a lot of useful information on their site. They have a big converted bus that they have done wonders with and made it fancy and functional. Spend some time on their website and you will soon know a lot more than most long-time RVers. New articles are posted every week and there are a lot of video interviews on this site that you will find interesting.

GoneWithTheWynns.com – Jason and Nikki Wynn have a website with a lot of in-depth articles and great information. They have articles and videos about how they make money while they're traveling, how they modified things on their RV, and they cover a lot of interesting places they have visited. Be sure to check out their website. (Update as of Jan. 2017: They sold their motorhome and are now living full-time on catamaran sailboat in the Caribbean, so their articles and videos now are about living on a sailboat, but you can still find a lot of interesting and useful RVing articles and videos on their website.)

RV-Dreams.com – Howard and Linda have a website that's full of information and personal experiences. Turn the TV off and spend a night reading and absorbing the wealth of information they have to offer. There is also a lively discussion forum on the site. You can find a link to their discussion forum in the left Nav. panel on their site.

InterstellarOrchard.com – Becky Schade is a 34-year-old, college educated, single female living full time in her RV. She does workamping and writing to fund her travels. On her site you can read her articles and you can learn more about what she does and her solo RVing lifestyle. She posts a couple of new articles every week and I think you will find them enlightening and interesting. Some of her articles are about her travels and some are about what she does, what she thinks and her life in general on the road as a full-time single female RVer.

CheapRvLiving.com – Bob Wells has a ton of information on his website about living in a van. He has lived in it full time and traveled for many years. He lives mostly on his

Social Security. Check out his website and see how he does it.

Motorhome.com/download-dinghy-guides – Some cars can be towed with all four wheels down and some require that you use a dolly. At this site for $1.99 they offer a downloadable guide, *The Guide to Dinghy Towing*. They have a different guide for each model year. If you already own a car you're considering towing, be sure to check your car's owner's manual to see if it can be towed with all four wheels down.

PplMotorhomes.com/sold/soldmenu.htm. – This site tells you what RVs have recently sold for. The people at PPL Motorhomes sell about 4,000 motorhomes a year and they show you what each one actually sold for. They also always have a huge inventory of used RVs for sale. Most of them are on consignment.

RVSchool.com – This is a great RV driving school. They teach you to drive in your own motorhome. Take a look at their schedule and see if they're going to be offering training at a rally near you. They offer substantial discounts at most RV rallies.

Use *Yelp.com* to find recommended local services— dentists, restaurants, auto repair shops, computer repair shops, etc.

There are thousands of good sources of information on the Internet (and, of course, thousands of sites with information that's not so useful). The links I have provided in this chapter are to the RVing resources (books, forums, videos, apps, and websites) that I use the most and the ones I think provide really useful information. I highly recommend you take a look at all of the resources I have linked to in this chapter and throughout the book.

If you have questions for me, feel free to email me at Jminchey@gmail.com or go to my website at **LifeRV.com** to learn more about the RV lifestyle and adventure. On the website you can post your questions in the discussion forum and you will get answers from me and other RVers.

As I've said many times in this book, whether you enjoy the RVing adventure or whether you find it frustrating will be determined a lot by your attitude. Spend some time watching the videos and reading the blogs that I've linked to in this chapter and I think when you realize how much fun other RVers are having and how much they are enjoying the adventure, it will help you realize how wonderful this lifestyle can be.

Bottom Line: If you're just starting out as an RVer (or considering becoming an RVer), realize that there is a lot to learn in order to safely and economically enjoy the RV lifestyle. Check out the links in this chapter and you will be well on your way to being an informed and experienced RVer.

Other Books by the Author

(You can find these books on Amazon.)

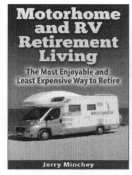
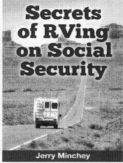
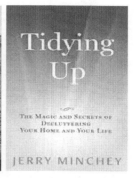

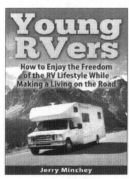

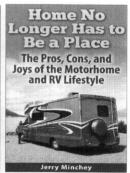

About the Author

"I can resist everything except temptation."

~ Oscar Wilde

Jerry Minchey is an electrical engineer, author, and business owner. He has a Bachelor's degree in Electrical Engineering, an MBA from USC, and an OPM degree from Harvard Business School. He worked for NASA and worked for many years as a computer design engineer. He has five patents and a private pilot's license with an instrument rating. He also enjoys playing old-time mountain fiddle music.

He has owned several engineering and marketing businesses. He is semi-retired now and is the founder and editor of the Internet subscription website **LifeRV.com**.

As an engineer and a business manager, he looks at problems from a logical standpoint as well as an economical and financial standpoint. He has written 11 books following this format of analysis and presentation.

He lives full time in his 34-foot Class A motorhome and spends the summer months in different places in the North Carolina Mountains and the winter months in Florida. He also makes several side trips throughout the year to music festivals, workshops, and to a rally or two when he finds one he likes. He says, "Home is wherever I park it."

####

Made in the USA
Middletown, DE
19 March 2017